To Thine Own Self Be True

To Thine Own Self Be True

BY

CORT R. FLINT

DROKE HOUSE, Publishers
ANDERSON, S. C.
No. 6736

TO THINE OWN SELF BE TRUE

Copyright©1968 by Cort R. Flint

First Edition

Library of Congress Catalog Card Number: 68-28780

Published by DROKE HOUSE, Publishers
1109 S. Main Street
Anderson, South Carolina

Manufactured In The United States Of America

Book Design by Lewis N. Schilling, Jr.

DEDICATED TO

O. C. Elliott
Henry Harrel
Dr. Mark F. Hawthorne
James A. Logan, Sr.
Dr. E. S. James
Dr. Forrest Maddox
T. Ree McCoy, Sr.
Elmer Perkins

who had the courage to be themselves

INTRODUCTION

Modern business has realized the greatest needs are not for better methods but for better men. Executives realize they cannot make, as their chief goal, the production of more and better materials, without having a sincere concern for their employees' emotional and spiritual health, which will produce, as a by-product, the increased efficiency, quality, and quantity that is desirable. The employer's interest is for the health, welfare, happiness, and security of his employees and for a type of product and service that benefits mankind. This has become the objective of the American business man. Some have failed this ideal but many more seek to attain this standard of excellence.

Some businesses have shown such a concern and have a chaplain to counsel in emotional, family, and personal problems so that each person can find a greater satisfaction in living and meaning to life.

Believing that everybody is somebody, they have sought to help each person find his particular place in life and the job for which he is best qualified in abilities and disposition. *This is done by helping one to be himself and to realize man's highest achievement is to be himself.* In any business that relies on personal service, a phony is spotted quicker than in other types of business. A phony salesman of a service or product raises questions as to whether the service or product is genuine.

Those from other nations and those with little knowledge of the business world are amazed at the ways that American business is providing leadership and concern for the complete development of their employees. Just as the medical profession and ministry work in teams of specialists, so does the world of business. The greatest assistance to people, in their daily problems, is often found in the surroundings provided by the employer.

Man's ego, pride, and self-esteem are closely related to his capacity for doing a job right. His strongest natural desire is to be successful, to achieve something worthwhile, and to feel he has value to his company, community, family, and religious affiliation. When this desire is frustrated, the employee is upset and manifests his discontent in everything he does.

Many men in management have learned to counsel with those who are going through the process of finding themselves in their particular work. In addition, industry has well-trained chaplains and other counselors who provide assistance in all the situations and crises that arise.

Psychologists and psychiatrists say that the chief frustration of this generation is hostility. Knowing this, many corporations search for avenues whereby frustrations may be resolved, enabling each person to be himself. They have found that providing an atmosphere for a man to be honest with himself enables him to be honest with others and frees him to be at his best in his work and all other relationships in life.

For a man to be honest with himself he must be aware of the four basic patterns of behaviour, instincts, and emotions that he has. These are: *sex, fear, anger, and wonder.* Many persons do not realize the importance of *wonder.* But it is in that behaviour instinct and emotion called *wonder* that lie all the beauty, art, drama, religion, and the highest aspirations of man. Also, man has seven basic desires that must be taken into account. The first, already mentioned, is to be successful. The others are: to be secure; to be accepted; to be appreciated; to be understood (the deepest desire); to be loved and to love and thus be of special worth to some person; (the greatest desire); and to have a meaningful life (the ultimate desire).

By understanding himself in relation to his emotions, which control 90% of his life, man can be at his best in his work, be true to himself, and discover the greatest joys and satisfactions of life.

Those who have experienced this exciting venture invite others to join them. Guidance is necessary so that the negative needs will be eliminated and the positive needs will be accentuated.

The road to health and happiness begins with faith that there is a God who is interested in every man's welfare. And integrity is the key to all enlightenment, understanding, and beneficial human relationships. Integrity begins by being honest with yourself, for the man who is honest with himself opens the way for honesty with all others.

CORT R. FLINT, Th. D.

PART I

TO THINE OWN SELF BE TRUE

Be yourself and think for yourself; and while your conclusions may not be infallible they will be nearer right than the concepts forced upon you by those who have a personal interest in keeping you in ignorance. You grow through making decisions, by reasoning, and through commitment. Only in exercising your faculties can you become a person. Claim your heritage that God has provided.

CHAPTER I

BEING YOURSELF – GREATEST LIKENESS

Never lose sight of this important truth: that no one can be truly great until he has gained a knowledge of himself, a knowledge which can only be acquired by occasional retirement.

– Zimmermann

Resolve to be thyself; and know that he who finds himself loses his misery.

– Matthew Arnold

Man is a mystery to himself. This deludes him into thinking he is a mystery to everybody else. Such a feeling is the basis for his greatest desire — that of being understood. Closely related to his desire to be understood is his wanting to be accepted. Self-understanding is necessary to his own well-being and emotional health. Such a foundation enables him to relate to others in a more meaningful way. How does all this begin? It starts by discovering the real person and by being true to that self.

Basically you have only one right — the right to be yourself. The joy of being yourself is life's greatest opportunity and an adventure that no one can afford to miss. The art of being yourself at your best is the privilege of unfolding the personality into the person you want to be. Biologists have stated that the possibility of even identical twins being completely alike is one chance to all the electrons in the world. Each person is an unique individual!

"Know thyself; know your strengths and your weaknesses; your relation to the universe; your potentialities; your spiritual heritage; your aims and purposes;" advised Socrates and then you will be able to "take stock of yourself." Taking stock requires patience, determination, and daily achievement.

First, there must be good treatment from your own hands — even being kind and gentle to yourself — being willing to forgive yourself, learning to love yourself, and then looking outward and finding how to have a right attitude toward others. A strong and wholesome self-esteem makes all things become new. Whatever you think about yourself that is negative, replace it by the belief that you were born to be a winner! There is a way that you can have the capacity, the knowledge, and the desire to develop your potential for the real self.

Such an assignment is a never ending struggle; but, it is when the going gets tough that the tough get going. The task is difficult but not impossible. The other side of the story is that the effort is worthwhile.

In relationships with other people, Shakespeare has given a wise axiom, "To thine own self be true, and it must follow, as the night the day, thou canst not then be false to any man."

There is a tiny spark in everyone that can be fanned into the flame of achievement.

The art of being yourself inspires the belief that you may begin to possess, at this very minute, those qualities of spirit and attitude that make for radiant living. It is accepting the philosophy of being yourself today, instead of becoming yourself in a tomorrow that never comes. Clement Stone has shown that a positive mental attitude can overcome the destruction of the negative mental attitude and bring out the best self — the true self.

In being yourself you can acquire courage, serenity, faith, hope, and love so that they can be expressed through you in everyday living.

There is one sense in which everyone has equal opportunity; it is in being true to one's real self — the only person that you can be. No greater admonition has been given to man than this: "To thine own self be true." Knowing God, self, and the purpose of life is the only fortune worth finding, and it is not to be found in faraway places — but in the heart itself.

The most outstanding quality of any person is his attitude or spirit. The key to any personality is the attitude or spirit he has toward God, people, self, and life. This attitude is determined by whether he is being true to his best self. Those who fail in life usually have a wrong spirit and attitude — often cynical toward life, hostile toward people, and doubtful about God. Such misfits have no contributions to make to their work, home, community, or religious group.

There are many calls and claims for one's time, talents, and life. But none is as important as the call of God — "To thine own self be true." Man's chief responsibility is to live his own life at its highest and best. *The cardinal sin is to fail in this responsibility.*

To be true to one's self is the highest aspiration. Objectively an experience is apparently good or evil; but subjectively, to the one who continues in fear and doubt, all is evil; to the one who trusts, all is good.

Many people feel they have had bad breaks which they cannot overcome. But past happenings that have damaged man's emotional life can be changed through the grace of God. Time must be taken, however, to understand the power of man's strongest drive in life – self preservation – and the four basic patterns of human behavior – sex, fear, anger, and wonder. This is a great age of intellectual pursuit, knowledge, and achievement. Yet man is rarely acquainted with himself and his emotions. Emotions control nine-tenths of man's actions. We must be aware of our emotions and why we act as we do if we are going to understand religion, fill our place in life, and have inner happiness and peace.

More than eighty per cent of the enlightenment in the fields of medicine, science, theology, and other areas has come in the last few years. With all of this knowledge, men still miss the one thing that is most important – the meaning of life – being in touch with the ultimate reality, which is called the love of God. The principle desire of man must be to know God, then to understand self, and to properly relate himself with people.

William James said that the wealth of any nation lies in the superior men that it develops.

An old German proverb states the responsibility of each generation: "As old birds sing, so young ones twitter."

There are only two philosophies of life. All other philosophies are in between these poles of expression. One was stated by Nietzsche in a threefold definition: the ultimate futility of human life; its transitional character, with no significance of its own; and one's personal acceptance of nothingness. The other was given through Christ – that life does have meaning, each life has a definite purpose, and this is revealed to each one in Christ. Those who have believed the latter have found a reason for living that brings inspiration and meaning.

If there is no God then it does not matter what one does with his life; but if there is a God nothing matters so much as knowing Him in personal relationship, knowing His will, doing His will, and being in His will. There is a purpose for every man's life as definite as for George Washington, Abraham Lincoln, Benjamin Franklin, and the Bible characters. Everybody is somebody in God's sight and is important in God's plan. To be true to the self that you were meant to be always *begins with willingness – the willingness to believe – the willingness to be.* Since man can never supply his basic needs, he must be willing for God to do for him what he cannot do for himself. Benjamin Franklin advocated the concept that God helps those who help themselves. This statement is true in some respects; but in the greater aspects of life, man can help everyone but himself. He must depend upon his fellow man and God for insight into himself. Only through the eyes of others is he able to see his blind spots and basic needs. Also, God is the only One who can bring the inner transformation that sets life in the right direction.

It is highly important, then, for you to become conscious of the self that God would have you to be. Everyone confronts two persons – the real self that God has predestined him to be and the role he is playing in life. Man can see this real self if his heart desires, and if he is willing to accept the means for his help.

Self-understanding is the beginning of man's deeper relationship to God and his higher behaviour and attitudes toward people

The Psalmist had insight into man's greatest needs:

"Trust in the Lord, and do good; Delight thyself also in the Lord; and he shall give thee the desires of thine heart. Commit thy way unto the Lord: trust also in him; and he shall bring it to pass. And he shall bring forth thy righteousness as the light, and thy judgment as the noonday."

The recognition of the real self comes through study, psychology, psychiatry, Bible reading, friends, group discussions, and heart-to-heart talking with someone who walks close to God. There is always much fear and trepidation in uncovering one's real self; the unknown is fearful. But bit by bit, as the genuine person begins to emerge, *the process becomes a fascinating adventure of wonder, anticipation, and joy from which you do not want to retreat.* There is only one person that any one can be; therefore, the deepest desire of the heart must lie in being the real self. All of the judgment of God, the love and happiness which can come to any one, is on the basis of whether he has been himself.

Most of the worries, unhealthy emotions, and sin that you permit in your life, befogging the way and limiting your true self, are caused by the unwillingness to let self be liberated through discipline and the power of God.

It is so easy to hold to foolish conventions, imagined necessities, and over-worn cliches. None of these belong to a self-emancipated human being. Nor do thoughts of violence, hatred, or destructive suspicions have a place in the healthy mind.

When self is emancipated there comes the joy and realization of the pricelessness of freedom. It is the natural state to which you have been born. Defective thinking and wrong teaching always lead to undesired designations. *The great men and women have been those who were not afraid to brush aside all the unhealthy traditions and unconfirmed facts.* These are the pioneers in freedom of thought and bold expression that have brought progress in all mental and spiritual enlightenment.

The example of Christ stands as the supreme representation of a self-emancipated life. His were eternal truths and those who have followed have found an open door to freedom from bondage. Therefore, a personal knowledge of God and a meaningful relationship with Him have made them free from the handicaps of the lesser self.

Life is difficult enough without the superfluous entanglements that you bring on yourself by being something less than your true self.

In being the true self you can become alive now; tolerant, happy, and in God's will.

The how and the why of being yourself will be revealed as you consider the step by step suggestions in this book. Begin with this challenge — You are not to live in conformity to someone else or some role. Be Yourself — Conformity is a crutch of mankind. Round pegs were not made for square holes.

Many men see things as they are and ask "why." I challenge you to see things that never have been in your life and ask "why not." Your potentialities are for you, and no one else can use them.

God has a meaningful life for you if you will accept it and seek to grow in the inner resources of being yourself.

Here are five suggestions to follow that will enable you to grow in understanding and help you to be true to yourself.

1. *Have a goal for your life.* The highest goal that you can have is to fulfill God's purpose for your life. The One who created you has a definite will for your life, and it is in this particular life that you find meaning, health, and happiness. Man must find goals that he believes in and then stay with them until they are realized to a large degree. Calvin Coolidge said:

> "Nothing in the world can take the place of persistence. Talent will not; nothing is more common than unsuccessful men with talent. Genius will not; unrewarded genius is almost a proverb. Education will not; the world is full of educated derelicts. Persistence and determination alone are omnipotent. The slogan 'Press On' has solved, and always will solve, the problems of the human race."

2. Have a plan to carry out the goal of your life. God has a blueprint for you that will unfold as you search for truth and enlightenment. Have a plan for your work. Work your plan.

This plan is a special pattern for your abilities, capacities, and uniqueness. God has not repeated his specific formation for any two people. There is no competition with someone taking your place. You are the only person that can be what you are to be and do.

3. Have a deep desire to carry out your goal that will leave you unsatisfied without the attainment of this goal. All great things start with a desire to be and to do. Remember the comforting promise of God's help: " . . . he shall give thee the desires of thine heart."

4. Commit your entire life without reservation. There can be a yearning and desire that never takes feet until you commit yourself to your goal.

5. Do not accept criticism from those who do not have an involvement in your goal. Sideline quarterbacks, who have never played the game, do not know the plays to call. Any team would be confused if they tried to carry out all the advice offered to

them.

A team usually wins the baseball game if they can get the opposing pitcher to have rabbit ears and throw away the game. A "rabbit-eared" pitcher lets the razzing and chatter of the crowd get the best of him.

Believe that the man who is honest with himself will have the capacity and basis to be honest with others. Out of such a man will come the greatest joys of life.

CHAPTER II

BEING YOURSELF – HOW DO YOU LOOK?

I study myself more than any other subject; it is my metaphysic, and my physic.

– Montaigne

Teach a wise man, and he will be wiser; teach a good man, and he will learn more.

– Kenneth N. Taylor
Paraphrased Proverbs 9:9

To be true to your real self depends upon how you look at yourself.

As you take a good look at yourself consider these words of Bernard: "Nothing can work me damage except myself; the harm that I sustain I carry about with me, and never am a real sufferer but by my own fault."

No outside force can permanently disturb, distress, or destroy. You determine your destiny by the response you give to truth and by how you apply this truth daily. You alone can decide what you let become a part of your life and beliefs.

If there was just one chapter in the Bible for you to read and understand, it would be the seventh chapter of Matthew. This chapter explains how to start living, how to commit your life to God, how to have the abundant and meaningful life, and ends with the benefits and consequences of making right and wrong choices.

In this chapter Jesus brings every human personality into the presence of God and unmasks him by revealing that everyone is a hypocrite or "play-actor" (the real meaning of the word hypocrite). Psychology and psychiatry have learned, through scientific research, that Jesus knew what he was talking about when he said *everyone was playing a role in life and needed to become a real person.*

In Greek drama the actor not only played the part assigned to him, but he wore a mask that portrayed the character. Those who have found a meaningful life and are free from the bondage of the past have removed the mask of the role they have been playing and have faced up to what they are in order that they may become what they are to be.

This is life's most difficult task — constantly facing what you are, dealing with unhealthy emotions, understanding why you act as you do, depending on someone else to give you guidance concerning your blind spots.

Therefore, start with your weakest personality defects and daily overcome them. You can become strongest on your weaker points. The deciding factor is your wanting to achieve your goal.

Through a thorough study, business has determined that the years 30 to 40 are the decisive ones for young men who hope to become major executives. The twenties are given to experimentation with different jobs, orientation to the commercial world, searching for the position he wants, and his goal in the business world. *This is parabolic of those who find life.*

Every young executive is faced with this question: How important are the rewards which achievement in a particular work will bring to me and my family? Am I willing to sacrifice a great deal of time, to devote myself unreservedly to this job and to work enthusiastically and diligently to make — not just a living — but a substantial success?

Every person faces this question in an emotional and spiritual sense. Each must ask himself if he is willing to give his complete life to God for the major overhauls that are necessary to keep his spiritual life at top performance, his timing in proper balance, and his tuning in harmony with God and his fellow man.

The answer to this question, also, must come from within man. Probably the greatest difficulty is that we are always planning to think about it, but never take time for this thinking. We want to do something about it, but never do. The consequence is that *we get an innoculation of religion which prevents us from getting a real dose.* We only get a taste of religion. Our problem is that we are trying to "get" religion on the run, but it will never happen; religion is absorbed in the quietness and solitude of life. Those who do not take time for it will never have it. The man who tries to save time in his religious growth only kills off his opportunity; it takes a lifetime to develop a spiritually mature personality.

First comes that painful experience of prying back the layers of life, much as you would peel an orange. The first look often causes one to cover up real fast. The ugliness that is bared is terrifying and your built-in self-defensive mechanism denies that it is you. But it is. Learning how this superficial self can be changed is the process we will be facing together. *That first look can be called the hell of self-discovery.*

Second comes the appropriation of the grace of God. *One mistake no one can afford is neglecting to receive the healing of God that is available.*

Man has a handicap that is difficult to overcome. We have the capacity to see the faults, sins, and mistakes of others, but we cannot see them in ourselves. An indication of your faults is what you despise in others. We must have the help of God and others to see our weaknesses. This is why Jesus said:

> "God will judge you in the same way you judge others, and he will apply to you the same rules you apply to others. Why, then, do you look at the speck in your brother's eye and pay no attention to the log in your own eye? — You imposter! (Hypocrite) Take the log out of your own eye first, and then you will be able to see and take the speck out of your brother's eye."

For abundant living no one can afford to be an actor, or, as the Bible calls such a person, a hypocrite. You must face the fact that *your biggest task is not to get ahead of others but to surpass yourself.*

The word "sin" has been misused so much that it has become meaningless to most people. But, since God selected this word to describe the barrier between man and Himself, we need to pause long enough to comprehend the word's true definition. *God's purpose is clearly marked.* His permissive will is seen in the process of man's development from where he has been, where everything is disorganized because of sin, to the place where he can be. Man is able through the indwelling spirit of God to distinguish between that which is vital and that which is secondary. He is enabled to see guilt as the failure to fulfill God's purpose for his life and all other guilts as false guilts. *Sin is, ultimately, having your way with your life rather than permitting God to have His way.*

To be true to one's self, you must overcome the habit of guiding yourself and enter into the better way by being guided through faith in a personal God whose methods are perpetual contradiction to man's every preconceived notion.

The meaningful and inspired life seeks to be obedient to the Spirit of God in all things and in every moment of life.

There are two aspects of your life of which you may not be aware. One is that, in all probability, you have a low esteem of yourself. This is true of almost every person who has not had some counseling or human relations training. The other is that you are lonely. We all realize that we are in bondage, but we make every effort to keep this hidden from others. We are constantly wrestling with estrangement, disunity, division, inadequacy, and separation. Paul Tournier has described this predicament of man as being in a state of tension between the need to reveal and the need to conceal. *Man is constantly looking for someone to whom he can reveal himself and be understood and, at the same time, be accepted.* There is a nagging fear that when the real person is seen no one will understand and also a fear of rejection. No one wants to empty his insides and have no benefit from such pain. Certainly one would not want to scare away those who are near and dear to him by dragging out the skeletons in his closet. Since the deepest desire in man is to be understood, he makes little progress until he finds someone who does understand.

The truth of the matter is that self must be revealed before low esteem will be overcome. A person who has understanding and empathy has an uncanny way of appearing in your life when you are receptive and ready to become your real self. So, instead of conversing superficially, as you feel the desire and need to divulge your true feelings, plunge into the depths of yourself and bring forth that which has been concealed and veneered even from you. Discussion about the change in the weather has seldom influenced anyone to be himself.

Again, referring to Swiss psychiatrist Paul Tournier and his *Meaning Of Persons,* he points out that every human being has a tendency to be a mysterious silence which constitutes an impenetrable retreat, a constant facile chit-chat, or to stay behind

abstractions, quotations, theories, and trivialities. This
shield from revealing his own opinion of himself. He h
inside and drawn back in fear at the task he faces. If son
could know this is the way everybody feels and is the
must pay for being a part of the human race.

Taylor Caldwell aptly describes man's greatest proble
basic needs are few and it takes little to acquire them
need, his most urgent need, is for someone to listen to
hear him out until he has spilled himself — to hear him as
being.

Your low esteem can change to love for the person
created to be.

The lonely person is closely related to low esteem.
alone and are lonely because you have never pulled
barriers, hindrances, and fear to let the real you speak up
completely, to someone.

Walking alone for many years and wanting to be un
when you are misunderstood does not help your situation
does a denial of your loneliness make the situation better.

This book keeps pointing the way. Train yourself to
message. Over and beyond this; listen to that other vo
keeps trying to get you to hear. This is the voice of
speaks to the inner man. Practice an awareness of God's
each day and you will be amazed at the turn your life take

CHAPTER III

BEING YOURSELF – HOW DO YOU LIVE?

It is pretty safe to presume that about all the glaring defects or petty weaknesses which we are looking for in others may with a little careful investigation be found in ourselves.

It is in immortalizing the present moment that your life may have eternal significance.

Jesus said that He came "that you might have life, and that you might have it more abundantly." The value of commitment to this life is that you do not waste time dreaming about the rich life you may live next year, or ten years from now. You can live at your best right now; God wants you to "live it up" all the time. For this to be a reality, you must be in touch with and receive the inner resources that come from this ultimate reality — God's love.

All of life is holy and is not to be dissipated. Jesus taught:

> "Do not give what is holy to dogs — they will only turn and attack you; do not throw your pearls in front of pigs — they will only trample them underfoot."

Life is to be lived in close relationship with God each day, in the faith that God will guide you through the day and supply your every need.

"A journey of a thousand miles begins with a single step," according to the wisdom of an ancient Chinese seer.

How we live depends upon *how we regard temptation*. When we are tempted, we will do one of three things. We can give over to the temptation and become its victim by entering into worldly lust, self-destruction, and other forms of self-indulgence. Or we can turn from the temptation on our own strength. Man has been led to think that when he has turned from temptation he has done the right thing. But this also is a wrong choice. God intends for man not to turn from temptation but to turn to Him in the temptation. By turning to God we find there is the power to cleanse and to destroy the temptation.

The gospel according to Luke gives a very dramatic picture of what happens when we depend upon our own strength to overcome temptation: "When an evil spirit goes out of a man, it travels over dry country looking for a place to rest; if it doesn't find one, it says to itself, 'I will go back to the house which I left'. So it goes back and finds the house clean and all fixed up. Then it goes out and brings seven other spirits even worse than itself, and they come and live with it. So that man is in worse shape when it is all over than he was at the beginning."

This is always the consequence of self-reformation. It has filled the churches with such self-righteous Pharisees that those from without look upon her as a sacred sorority for the snubbing of sinners. Such people make of their own religion a moralistic code rather than an abundant, joyous life. Their goal is to rule or ruin. Rather than being a choice of either-or, they do both — rule and ruin.

The Biblical concept that man is tempted by a power of evil within himself has produced people who have fought against sin and has caused them to trust in the power of God to do for them what man cannot do for himself. The modern idea of blaming man's heredity and his circumstances for his sin has produced people who succumb at once to sin and remain in its power. Their disillusioned and unhappy lives have brought depression to themselves and the world.

The Holy Spirit is the only One who can detect the temptations; neither common sense nor human wisdom can recognize them as temptations. Temptations always seek to make man want to be the master of his life rather than to let God be the Master.

In facing temptation one must go beyond prayer and the Bible to the person — the subject of prayer and the Bible — the living God. He will apply the word of God to the individual, and the temptation will cease. Wise is the person who grows through his temptations, but "like a dog that returns to his vomit is a fool that repeats his folly." God destroys the sin within and the temptation at each step when one turns the temptation over to Him.

How we live also depends *upon how we regard truth*. We must recognize the truth that God's purpose for life is to make us holy. People often think that repentance is God's standard for man. God's standard for man is not repentance, but holiness. Jesus came not to teach man but *to give man a totally new heredity,* and the Sermon on the Mount describes how that heredity will work out. There is a calm deliberation about the injunctions in the Sermon on the Mount. We are not asked to obey them until the Holy Spirit brings them to remembrance. We are told to commit ourselves to God who will bring us the inner life, spirit, and attitude described in the Beatitudes, and applied in the rest of Matthew 5-7.

Every individual shrinks at the truth about himself. He is afraid of his inferiorities, of what is buried deep in his life which he has never faced. One realizes, when these shadows are once recognized that they will have to be dealt with in some way. *The constant inward nagging that people face every day is the real self demanding its place.* Some recognize this in their spirit of restlessness and deep dissatisfaction.

Man's baser nature revolts against the change that truth challenges him to make. There is always the basic fear of the unknown. Since fear is one of man's basic patterns in human behavior, he will want to run away from what he is confronting. Such primitive action has enabled man to preserve his physical life. However, to run would spoil his opportunity for freedom. Another impulse from fear is to seek to control the situation and the truth. This, also, would be disastrous. In such fear man must turn to God for the power to overcome fear. The Bible teaches "God does not give you a spirit of fear, but of power, and of love, and of a sound mind."

In such a crisis human nature does not want to accept the fact that true education calls for self-transformation. Rather, man's basic nature wants to accomplish life's purpose through the mere assimilation of propositional forms of truth, and the theory that the themes of death and resurrection are for verbal dissemination, not for personal assimilation. However, *religion is always personal* and not propositional.

"As in water, face answers to face, so the mind of man reflects the man."

39

The truth is in a person. Jesus said, "I am the way, the truth, and the life."

How we live depends upon how we regard temperance. *Temperance is always in conflict with self-indulgence.* This quality not only applies to the way we treat our bodies, but also to our spirit and attitude toward other people and self. There is a great need for all people to love each other and respect each other. It is difficult to give people the right to believe or disbelieve in their own manner and way. Man is so prone to take over the prerogative of God by taking away man's personal privilege to think for himself. People are not inclined to think for themselves. The others are controlled. A truly religious person can never employ manipulation to cause people to agree with him. Agreement must be in the heart.

When any person lives in any extreme attitudes and way of life, he has lost contact with the centrifugal force of God's will and purpose. The mature person seeks harmony in church fellowship that is the direct result of the leadership of the Holy Spirit.

It is of much importance that no person judge any man in an unjust spirit. When he is inclined to criticize, he must recognize the spirit of criticism as the sin which concerns him, and not the behaviour of another.

Temperance, as used in this context, means being in the center of God's will and going in the direction of His purpose, rather than running from one extreme to the other.

CHAPTER IV

BEING YOURSELF – HOW DO YOU LOVE?

Love one human being purely and warmly, and you will love all. – The heart in this heaven, like the sun in its course, sees nothing, from the dew drop to the ocean, but a mirror which it brightens, and warms and fills.

– Richter

To be true to one's self is related to how one learns to love.

The old song declares: "You're Nobody 'Til Somebody Loves You; You're Nobody 'Til Somebody Cares." This is true!

We all tend to think we are experts in the area of love. A person may be 9 or 99 — yet whatever the age, there is a tendency to overestimate one's capacity in love. Love is a capacity and must be realized in its overall purpose to heal and make well.

Some years ago, Billy Hill wrote a song and described this love between man and woman. Some of the words were:

> True love can never die;
> Nothing else ever mattered
> Only a love that's true.
> You have to give a little, take a little,
> And let your poor heart break a little.
> That's the story of, that's the glory of love.
> As long as there's the two of us
> We've got the world and all its charm.
> And when the world is through with us,
> We've got each other's arms.

These words seem sentimental for this cynical age, but they aptly describe what some men and women have shared in the story and glory of love.

As Jesus was entering the close of His earthly ministry, He told His disciples: "A new commandment I give you: love one another. As I have loved you, so must you love one another."

43

Multitudes are starved for love, understanding, and acceptance.

The purpose of every life is to be filled with God's love and to respond with love in all situations of life. The only ethic that Jesus taught was to react toward people with love in every circumstance.

There are four kinds of love that God provides for people.

There is physical love, which is usually referred to as "being in love." This love is what the Greeks called *eros,* the love of the man and woman who commit themselves to each other and to none other. No man or woman can be complete until this love has come into the heart. God will lead you to the right person to marry. That is why it is so important to wait for that one who brings true love.

This love between a man and a woman can be frustrated to despair, divorce, and destruction unless sex is understood. Sex is who you are, not what you do. *The persons who relate to each other are the important parts of sex.* Much emphasis is given to methods of sex relations, how to improve them, and how to adjust in sex. These are important, but not nearly so important as the person being salvaged from selfishness, indulgence, and immaturity. The bondage to the inner child of the past and the failure to resolve these emotional binds are the real causes for marriage failures.

A second love, parental and child, which the Greeks called *storge,* or affection, describes the feelings that one has for his family. In this love people are drawn together as a distinctive unit of devotion. Family love can bring stability, security, understanding, and the right foundations for a happy life. How children are guided in these early years of toilet training, emotional behavior, and sexual development will largely determine their adulthood.

Another type of love is the partnership that brings friends together in their common concern and interests. Friendship is born at the moment one person says to another, "What! You too? I thought that no one but myself ... " Friends are able to bare their personalities to each other. *Friendship is uninquisitive; each person is simply what he is.* The Greeks had a word for this — *philia. A friend is one who knows all about the person and still loves him.*

This beautiful poem describes the inspiring love of a friend.

"I love you, not only for what you are, but for what I am
    when I am with you.
I love you, not only for what you have made of yourself, but
    for what you are making of me.
I love you for the part of me that you bring out.
I love you for putting your hand into my heaped-up heart and
    passing over all the frivolous and weak things that you
    cannot help seeing there and drawing out into the light
    all the beautiful, radiant things that no one else looked
    quite far enough to find.
I love you for ignoring the possibilities of fool in me,
    and for laying firm hold of the possibilities of good
    in me.
I love you for closing your eyes to the discords in me and
    for adding to the music in me by worshipful listening.
I love you because you are helping me to make of the lumber
    of my life, not a tavern, but a temple, and of the words
    of my days, not a reproach, but a song.
I love you because you have done more than any creed could
    have done to make me happy.
You have done it without a touch, without a word, without a
    sign.
You have done it by being yourself.
After all, perhaps this is what being a friend means."

The fourth, and deepest love, is *agape*. It has many applications and ways of expressing itself.

Members experience the participating love found in the fellowship of the church. Whenever one meets a person who has come to know God in a personal relationship, he feels at home. He has met another individual who is under the guiding Spirit of God. There is nothing in human relationships that is as meaningful and helpful as to be of one heart and one mind in the Christian fellowship. Here we learn to be obedient to God's Spirit and to acknowledge God in all that is done and said.

The real meaning of *agape*-love is *"unconquerable benevolence"*. If one is regarded with *agape*, it means that nothing that that person can or will ever do will cause one to seek anything but his highest good. It is through this love that God has built His hopes and plans for the world. In this fellowship God reveals the reality of redemption, forgiveness, and love. This love enables people in the church to take time to know each other, help each other, and stand by each other. It provides an *atmosphere where one can reveal himself rather than continue to conceal himself.*

Those who are keenly aware of what God has done for them, have a particular love for those outside their own group. In theological terms this is called *compassion.* It is the desire that loved ones, friends, and all whom one knows, will come to know God and have the redemptive life. This is characteristic of all those who are committed. They want everyone to know God. Life is dedicated, money is given, and time is used in such a way that a good witness of what God has made possible in Christ can be seen and understood.

Another aspect of *agape* which is seldom realized, but which God has planned for everyone, is perfect love. This love is to be applied in all relationships. It is particularly missing with close loved ones.

Families notice the need for this love when a child is born into the world. The parents want to give this baby the best things in life. They surround the child with their love and with things. Then they realize that something is missing. The baby needs perfect love. This perfect love can only come from God. Therefore they must learn to pray, "God, love this child through us."

Perfect love can never be manipulated or reduced by man in any way. The only thing man can do is to be a channel for that love. As the perfect love of God flows through him to others, it is as a mountain stream carrying gold; deposits of gold are left along her banks and leave them greatly enriched. The other areas of love are never adequate since they are hindered by becoming a part of man's interpretation and action. They become enriched when every person begins to pray for God to love his wife, his children, through him. Families are cheated when the members leave off the perfect love of God flowing through them in all their relationships. God's perfect love, going through the devout each day, transforms the life more than any other aspect of the religious life. One begins to look at people in the love that God has for him. When one becomes disgusted or upset with the family or close friends, he needs the perfect love of God flowing through him to set lives straight and to bring all things in order.

Love is such a power that it unites all things. Therefore, love God, and everything that He has will be yours.

CHAPTER V

BEING YOURSELF – HOW DO YOU LAST?

Persistent people begin their success where others end in failure.

– Edward Eggleston

Victory belongs to the most persevering.

– Napoleon

Perseverance and audacity generally win.

– Deluzy

The only failure a man ought to fear is failure in cleaving to the purpose he sees to be best.

– George Eliot

How one lasts depends upon who controls his life. Jesus said, "If any man will come after me, let him deny himself, and take up his cross daily, and follow me."

This simply means that man is to get off the throne of his life and let God take over the throne of his life. Then man begins to receive the daily power of God. The art of receiving is man's most ardent task. His capacity to receive is enlarged by desire and appropriation.

In the Sermon on the Mount, Jesus gives the basis for man's lasting faith: "Ask, and it shall be given you; seek, and ye shall find; knock, and it shall be opened unto you: For every one that asketh receiveth; and he that seeketh findeth; and to him that knocketh it shall be opened."

How one lasts depends upon how hard he works at his convictions, his devotion to God, and the determination of his courage. Thomas A. Edison said that there were three essentials to achieve anything worthwhile – hard work, stick-to-itiveness, and common sense.

As Jesus gave instructions to the apostles as they went out to preach, He told them that those who endured unto the end would be saved. There is a faith which lasts through the trials, doubts, testings, difficulties and sorrows every mature person faces. This kind of faith is a gift of God in accordance with the true desires of the heart. The difference in Peter and Judas was the quality of their faith.

This depends upon where we get our information.

No person can grow in the plan of God for his life until he is willing to accept the discipline of study, prayer, and sharing in the heartfelt fellowship. This is never easy because the natural man, that is always with every person, rebels against the daily schedule of prayer, Bible reading, study of religious books, and sharing in depth fellowship. Many people have gone through life waiting for the time to come when they would feel like taking on these aspects of a meaningful life. That time never comes. God does not discipline people so that they will seek this information. The discipline must come from self.

If one spends all of his time with the information that the world gives he will never understand what God seeks to bring to man. Jesus said: "Peace I leave with you, my peace I give unto you: not as the world giveth, give I unto you. Let not your heart be troubled, neither let it be afraid."

This depends upon where we get our inspiration. When we examine the motivation of our lives we get a good picture of what we are.

Europe, even to a larger degree than the United States, has suffered the tragic effects of people seeking to build life upon personal pleasure and the material things of life. Individuals have come to such a low state in neuroses that psychiatrists there have been leading in a new approach in their efforts to help humanity. Dr. Paul Tournier for many years led in seminars with doctors, laying upon their hearts the necessity for bringing one's personal relationship to God into their counseling. His book, *"The Meaning of Persons"* should be in every home. In the first part of the book he shows how psychiatry and psychology can help one to see the role he is playing in life and something of the real person. The second division deals with the insight one gets through introspection. The third portrays the healing that comes through our dialogue with God. The world-renowned Dr. Viktor E. Frankl has introduced a new word — "Logotherapy" — into the doctor's vocabulary. Logotherapy extends the frontiers of psychiatric knowledge and insight by introducing the concept of "the will to meaning" in life and emphasizing its role in the treatment of neuroses. Previous psychiatric approaches to the neurotic personality have seriously neglected man's spiritual values in favor of the basically materialistic drives embraced by the pleasure principle of the will to power. It is Dr. Frankl's chief aim to redress the balance by emphasizing the existence of man's need to be in a right relationship to God and developing a psychiatric approach (known as existential analysis) for ministering to man's frustrations. More than ever before in human history, Dr. Frankl contends, the unrequited quest for meaning in life is the cause of neurosis. It was during his years in the notorious concentration camp of Auschwitz, and the immediate postwar years in Europe, that this psychiatrist observed the close kinship between individual striving for fulfillment and the essentially religious yearning in man.

Man can gain a certain amount of inspiration from his own achievements in business, the social world, politics, lust, and power. But all these become ashes and he finds himself alone and afraid because this kind of inspiration cannot supply his deepest needs.

This depends upon where we get our sense of integrity.

Integrity is the basic word for life and the basic quality in life. Integrity is a gift of God, but it never comes to those who do not want it. Integrity begins with a person being willing to be honest with himself.

When General Dean was a captive during the Korean War, one of his interrogators told him that he had a few minutes to write a farewell note to his family. General Dean had no reason whatsoever to believe he would ever have any chance to say any other word to any member of his family. He had no way of knowing the letter would ever be delivered, but he was morally certain that in less than thirty minutes he would be taken out of his little cabin and shot. What, under those circumstances, would you write to your only son?

There are only eight or nine lines of his letter, but right in the middle of the letter General Dean said, *"Tell Bill the word is integrity."* What would you say under the circumstances? Tell Bill the word is "popularity?" Tell Bill the word is "security"? Tell Bill the word is "happiness"? The word General Dean chose is a bigger one than all the others. "Tell Bill," he said, "the word is integrity."

No man is by nature honest with himself. He would rather live in a world of pretense than risk the ordeal of the daily searching, in the presence of the Holy Spirit, as to who he is and the willingness to be transformed into what God would have him to be.

In a sense, integrity is the beginning and the end. God's redemption begins with man being honest enough to admit the guilt and sin that separate him from God and his being willing for God's will to be his will. As God's Spirit melts down the qualities of man in his deception, pretense, littleness and manipulation, He places in their stead that wonderful quality of integrity.

Dr. Karen Horney has observed that the first and best prize of coming to the real self is that *the real self is strong and even more capable than the phony one.* Along with this genuine strength comes a realization of the need for vigilance and suspicion, and eventually a sense of oneness with God begins to bloom life into its orbit of joy and meaningfulness. Coming into such a realm brings an end to the need to fight, manipulate, avoid or seduce everyone. Self-contempt disappears, along with permitting abuse and the seeking of power. *It becomes possible to be wholehearted, make decisions, take consequences, respect others, and be spontaneous without pretenses.*

Being true to self is pictured in the story that has been called the Parable of the Prodigal Son. This narrative of a boy who rebelled against the love of his father and wanted to run his own life gives a pointed illustration of one who is not true to his own self. Everyone has some of this prodigal in dreams or experience.

People in their twenties seem to be an extension of adolescence or, even more likely, of childhood. During this age period there are multi-personalities which may not at all resemble their true self. One can at this stage even imagine himself infallible. He is certainly very critical of the ignorance of adults and their incapacity to understand.

During their thirties many people begin to find themselves and like the prodigal, when he came to himself, start in the right direction. Fate and circumstances may have cheated him out of a good start but man can now learn self acceptance and begin to be the person that God desires. Those who make it — to become the real self — do so by their forties. By this time a person has rid himself of the need to be mothered and the compulsion to manipulate and dominate.

Everyone finds his own peculiar and particular method which is unique and unrepeatable. Underneath what is done is the commitment to give all yourself to God's purpose and to have a more useful and loving life. Carl Jung defined personality as the state toward which a man is growing: not the transient being he is, but what he is planning to make of himself. Anyone who wishes his life to improve must learn that unless a man changes, invariably he will never make it. This is of God. Where the heart is willing, it will find a thousand ways for personal growth; but where it is unwilling, it will find a thousand excuses.

To thine own self be true! You will have a great time doing it.

SOME THOUGHTS FOR YOUR CONSIDERATION

1. Do you see the faults in the other person, but never face up to yourself?

2. Do you tend to blame others for your situation, rather than accepting responsibility for what you are now and what you can be? You will be what you truly want to be. To learn, you must want to be taught.

3. There is a great potentiality in you that is related to the real self that you are to be. Your biggest task is not to get ahead of others, but to surpass yourself.

4. You hold the key as to whether you will harness the inner powers God has within you.

5. What you see of the barriers to your health and happiness can be eliminated by positive thinking, accepting the help of God and acting on the highest and best course for each day. Try Clement Stone's idea of letting the Positive Mental Attitude overcome the Negative Mental Attitude.

6. *The most important living person is yourself.* This is the person for whom you have the most responsibility — to accept the avenues for your becoming your real self.

7. *God is working with you to help you become the real self.*

8. There is no valley of depression that you can not cross. There is no mountain that you can not climb to become the real self.

9. Every disappointment, adversity and heartache can be turned to aid you by making this an inner dissatisfaction.

10. Don't let your pattern of thinking or action make you a "has been." It is not the number of times you fall, but how often you get up that really counts. *You are what you think.*

11. All things are possible to those who believe.

12. You were born to be a victor not a victim. Identify with those who have succeeded. You have the inner capacities for surmounting any and every obstacle. The touch of God in the inner man brings them to life, power, and action.

PART II

YOU BET YOUR LIFE

Every man's life is a plan of God.

— Horace Bushnell

Life will give you what you ask of her if only you ask long enough and plainly enough.

— E. Nesbit

A wise youth makes hay while the sun shines, but what a shame to see a lad who sleeps away his hour of opportunity.

— Kenneth N. Taylor
Paraphrased Proverbs 10:5

CHAPTER VI

IT'S YOUR LIFE YOU ARE BETTING

If this life be not a real fight, in which something is eternally gained for the universe by success, it is no better than a game of private theatricals from which one may withdraw at will.

— William James

The more mature person knows that something must be done to help 95 per cent of their acquaintances to get past the baby stage of life. Many people appear hypocritical because they talk about experiences which they have never known personally. What can be done to lead them to a more meaningful life which gives off the reality of God within human life? How can they have an understanding of God and self that will enable them to give a different picture? What can be done to get people to quit talking in generalities and be specific? Before one can get very far in this regard *he must know the difference between intellectual and emotional acceptance.* One can accept the idea of God without ever accepting a personal God to transform and direct his life. *Emotional* means to get something down into the heart where it produces a difference in spirit, attitude and behavior.

Consider again the seventh chapter of Matthew. Often this passage of Scripture is considered as emphasizing the negative aspects of life because of Jesus' statement that man must see his own faults before helping others. Nothing could be further from the truth. This is the apex of the Sermon on the Mount. It is the mountain peak which one seeks to ascend so that all of life might fit into its proper focus. Jesus is showing that before one can begin anything in life he must first take up the matter of himself. The wise Seneca wrote, "Other men's sins are before our eyes; our own are behind." *One of life's greatest difficulties is that too many people tend to everybody's business but their own.*

Man's chief responsibility is to rid his life from unhealthy emotions and be himself, the self which God intends for him to be. Each must accept the fact that *his primary job is to live his own life.*

When the world defines success it considers someone who has invented a new gadget, discovered a scientific formula, achieved materialistic success, written great literature, shared generously with humanity, or shared physical suffering. This is not the true concept of greatness. God discloses through His record that man is successful only when he has self-understanding — a knowledge of who he is, his destiny in life and his place of service.

Everyone remembers the popular television program called "You Bet Your Life." Whether one is aware of it or not, every person is betting his life on what he believes and how he lives.

In the fifth chapter of The Acts of the Apostles there is the story of a man by the name of Ananias and his wife Sapphira. They bet their lives that the truths these first Christians were telling were false. They saw people who seemed to be highly emotional and very dedicated to a cause getting something great out of life. Upon examining what was taking place in their lives, they decided there was nothing to it, that these people were just making up the story they were telling about what God had done in their lives and what God had meant to them. Because of this they put it to a test and found out that it was true. Both of them sold out their lives in this world and the world to come because they bet their lives that there was no reality to the indwelling of God's Spirit within the human personality. *They would not believe that God spoke directly to man.*

As Jesus leads individuals to the crucial point of personal discernment, He tells them that they must get the big piece of timber out of their eyes before they can ever help anyone else who has a splinter or speck of sawdust in his eye. Jesus used the word *mote,* which in the Greek means a little splinter, and the word *beam,* which in the Greek means rafter. In other words, the most important thing is *to thine own self be true.* Years before Christ, a Greek philosopher by the name of Socrates had said that the most important thing for man was to know himself. "Know thyself" was counted one of the oracles of the Greeks. It was inscribed as one of their three great precepts, in letters of gold, on the temple of Delphi and was regarded as divine. Modern psychology and psychiatry have added much to the dimension of man's knowing who he is. Mature people welcome this help, for this is a part of the truth that God has to reveal to every individual. The beginning of all true experiences of life, emotional health and faith is for one to know himself. Jesus said, "Blessed are the poor in spirit: for theirs is the kingdom of heaven." This is one who recognizes who he is and who God is. He knows he cannot help himself. He realizes that he cannot change himself; that he must depend upon God to do what he cannot do for himself. However, the right beginning has meaning only if one is able to follow through in the pace of life to make a good ending. Those who have run the mile race know that one not only has to make a good beginning of the race and pace himself through the race, but he also has to have a good finish. That is why Jesus said that the one who endured to the end would be the people of God. Such a person has found a quality of life that brings him through each day.

Each person must decide how he is going to bet his life in the circumstances of this day. The Nineteenth Century put an exclamation mark to the world. The Twentieth Century has placed a question mark to everything that is said and done.

Everyone must determine how he is going to use his life. Actually, he chooses whether he will invest his life or squander it. The vogue of the day is to try to make the prodigal son comfortable in the "far country" without getting him out of the far country. This will not work. Man must see himself as he is – inadequate, undone, and lost.

No man ever made an ill figure who understood himself, nor a good one who mistook himself.

Each person then, must begin where he is, with what he has, to make of life what it is.

God created man with a desire for freedom. But he cannot be free until another act of God makes him free. The cost to man is that he give up all rights to himself and commit his life and the control of it into the hands of God. Freedom is costly to those who make it possible for others. A good example is seen in the lives of those who signed the Declaration of Independence.

The night before the Declaration of Independence was adopted, John Adams of Massachusetts wrote his wife, "I am well aware of the toil and blood and treasure it will cost us to maintain this Declaration."

His 55 co-signers were equally aware of the danger and prepared to pay any price. Pay they did:

Richard Stockton of New Jersey was betrayed, dragged from his bed and thrown into prison by the enemy. He died prematurely, at 51, broken in health by his mistreatment in prison.

Lyman Holt and George Walton of Georgia suffered confiscation of property and imprisonment, respectively.

William Whipple of New Hampshire had his leg shattered by a cannonshell at the Battle of Rhode Island. A few months later, with a wooden leg, he was back in Congress.

John Morton of Pennsylvania died eight months after signing the Declaration, ostracized by relatives and friends.

John Hart of New Jersey was driven from the bedside of his dying wife, his 13 children were scattered, his 400-acre farm was destroyed by fire and he was forced, at 65, to live as a fugitive for a year and a half.

Francis Lewis of New York had his home ransacked and burned. But far worse, his wife was taken prisoner and locked in a squalid jail. As a result of harsh treatment, she died within two years.

To free man to live is costly. It requires constant discipline, continued growth, certain study and conflicting determination. It can be done only in fellowship with others. Man has been fashioned in such a manner by his God that he is dependent upon other people for this change.

Some very definite goals are given to the man as he starts his pilgrimage in life. He can listen or go on his own. However, he must always remind himself, "This is my life that I am betting."

CHAPTER VII

THINK AS YOURSELF

All truly wise thoughts have been thought already thousands of times; but to make them truly ours, we must think them over again honestly, until they take root in our personal experience.

— Goethe

Oftentimes nothing profits more than self-esteem, grounded on what is just and right.

— Milton

Creative thinking is nothing more and nothing less than being first.

EVERY PERSON MUST BEGIN WITH THINKING *AS HIMSELF*.

He must dare to have ideas and opinions, no matter how unpopular. A psychiatrist has said that he has largely quit attending professional medical symposiums which should be keeping him up on the developments in his field because so few of the experts attending them ever really said anything. He went on to add, "They're all so afraid of offending somebody that they hedge, they qualify, they straddle fences until there's nothing left but mush." It is a great truth that those who straddle the fence never get their feet on the ground. Billy Graham has described a mugwump as a person who has his mug on one side of the fence and his wump on the other.

There is one knowledge which is every person's duty and interest to acquire and that is self-knowledge. Else to what end was man endowed by the Creator with the faculty of self-consciousness? No other animal was so endowed.

The malaise of these days is "dislocation of the self." Everyone seems to be going about improving social conditions, environment, schools, take-home pay and recreational facilities, convinced that they will produce happy and noble human beings. Nobody would advocate deprivation that scars the ego, but the alternative of losing the individual self in circumstances and possessions leaves people hungry and thirsty for something that they have not experienced.

Man is not by nature an individualist or even a person. He is lost in the mass of humanity and engrossed in the world of things. He belongs so completely to his group that he is without personal autonomy. His conformity has robbed him of his real self. If this is not his case, he goes to the other extreme of having such total autonomy that he becomes an isolated individual, who has no communication with others.

Another dilemma of man is seen in the United States where many people are caught between the old Puritan notion of self as inherently evil, and the Freudian idea that self is compounded of external experiences. One still urges people to be selfless; the other, to get as much self as possible — only it will have to come from others who may not be disposed to give it.

This is very awkward. One in such a circumstance can neither look forward nor backward. He wanders a waste-howling wilderness, looking for ways to stand as an individual, as though he were something to be endured until he got the hang of melting away or wooing an identity from others. The old law, shocking as it sounds to modern ears, goes so far as to commend loving self. One must constantly remind himself that Jesus said, "Thou shalt love thy neighbor as thyself." It is important to note that this is not "in the place of" — which clearly implies a right to proper self-appreciation and more than a right, an obligation.

Love of others begins in decent self-esteem. If one doesn't believe in his own entity, he can't very well give it to others in love, in work, in service, or in anything else. All people who have meant anything to the world have been those who, far from effacing the self, cherished and utilized it, commanded it, trained it, freed it and enjoyed it. Yes, even the saints. Bitterness and defeat come from non-use of the power that is within the individual which he seeks to bring out into a true personality. Frustration comes from the abilities being stifled in an unrealized self.

Milton wrote, "Oftentimes nothing profits more than self-esteem, grounded on what is just and right."

One could hardly imagine Abraham Lincoln declining to run for president on the grounds of its being vain and glorious, or Sir Winston Churchill, Mrs. Eleanor Roosevelt, Babe Ruth, Charles Lindbergh, John Glenn, Florence Nightingale, Chopin, Beethoven, or Wagner waiting around for somebody else to point out their paths or personality. It is true that these people were particular, but so is each person. No one is a mask-man; a puppet. Each is somebody in particular. The question is — WHO? How shall one discover himself with the ones with whom he is to come in touch?

In a day of much conformity and so little courage, how important it is for the church and community to see their mission to youth — that they can think as themselves. Socrates, when he returned to Rome, asked and was told about the young people. Someone queried him, "Why do you ask about youth instead of the affairs of state and what was going on in the world?" "Because, as go the young people," he replied, "so go the world in the days to come."

Benjamin Kidd put it like this: "Give us the young and we'll create a new mind and a new world in a generation."

A man's first care should be to avoid the reproaches of his own heart; his next, to escape the censures of the world.

This is the road for any person to think *as* himself.

To think as himself is necessary for anyone to be real. Any other way is counterfeit, superficial and a miserable substitute. In the human personality there is no substitute for the real thing — the real person.

Responsibility and authority from the human viewpoint rest in each individual. One must decide within himself. In this light he must ask himself whether he has ever said *yes* to life — whether he has ever started being himself — whether he has ever let the real joys of life pour into him.

Life is offered to everyone. Each person can accept or reject it. God intends for all to have an abundant life. The choice is to live or just exist. This was the choice Jesus gave to His home town of Nazareth. Sin causes people to be blind. Wrong choices cause the sin that brings blindness. Because of this everyone needs to have a better understanding of God and His offer to mankind.

"What does God do all day?" once asked a small boy. One could wish that more adults would ask so vital a question.

It does not occur to most men and women that God is engaged in any particular work in the world anymore than it occurs to a little child that his father does anything except be his father. He may be a bank president, a doctor, an electrician, a pastor, a businessman, a weaver, or a builder, but to this master-egoist he is *father,* and nothing more. Childhood, in one sense of the word, is the great self-centered period of life.

But as clearly as there comes to the growing child a knowledge of his father's part in the world, and a sense of what real life means, there must come to every person, whose growth is true a larger view of God's purpose for mankind. Next to losing the sense of a personal God, the worst evil that can befall any person is to have no sense of anything else. To grow up in complacent belief that God has no business in this great groaning world of human beings except to attend to a few saved souls is the negation of all religion. The first great epoch in a religious life, after the awe and the wonder of its dawn, is when there breaks into one's consciousness some sense that God has a definite purpose for every person, a purpose beyond him and his needs, beyond the churches and their creeds, beyond Heaven and its saints — a purpose which embraces every man and woman, every boy and girl, every nation, every race — a purpose which is concerned not with one's spiritual growth alone but with his personality in every part, his progress, his health, his work, his salary and his happiness in this present world.

What, then, does God do all day? He does not sit in church buildings waiting for people to come and worship Him. He is everywhere, with every person, to give direction and joy to life and the religious aspirations flowing from the heart of all mankind.

This world is an unfinished one. It is not wise; it is not happy; it is not pure; it is not good; it is not sanitary.

Jesus announced to the people in his home town the purpose of His coming into the world and tried to get them to see their neglect of and disobedience to God. When He pointed to people, outside his own, who had been obedient when they had not, they became angry and would have killed Him. This is too often the reaction of people to truth and life. They cannot comprehend it, so they seek to destroy it.

"Did you ever?" could be asked concerning many things. Did you ever get mad over some trifle? Did you ever eat too much? Did you ever think you were in love and then find out you were not? But there is a big question that needs to be asked: "DID YOU EVER SAY YES TO LIFE?"

Every man is in a shell until he desires to be different. The daily struggle of going from one stage of enlightenment and change to another enables process and progress to take place.

Every person must learn that he does not attain goodness by "straining every nerve" to become spiritual by his own efforts. One does not come to righteousness by seeking God's favor, but by responding to His love.

THE CHOICE IS UP TO EACH INDIVIDUAL.

No one can afford to drift into life. Drifting leads through the wide gate to destruction of personality and life. Jesus said, "Go in through the narrow gate, for wide and easy is the road that leads to hell, and there are many who travel it. The gate is narrow and the way is hard that leads to life, and few people find it."

Some time ago a woman was invited to speak before a large woman's club and tell them the secret of her happy life. She received a glowing introduction in which the presiding officer asserted that many envied her radiant personality and abundant life. She rose and began to speak.

"I am afraid I am going to startle you when I tell you that a tramp changed my life." Immediately you could have heard that proverbial pin drop. She continued, "I was washing the breakfast dishes one morning when there came a knock at the back door. I opened it and saw a tramp standing there. Very politely and very deliberately he took off his hat and bowed.

"'Madam,' he said, 'I am ashamed to beg. I have tried to find work but have failed. I will gladly work for my breakfast, for I am very hungry. Is there something that you have that I can do?'"

"I stood there and looked down at him with my arms akimbo and told him in pretty severe tones that I had no patience with tramps and that I never gave them anything. I added, 'You can tell your fellow tramps to stay away from my back door. I work for my living, and you can work for yours. I will not feed you.' When he stood there without moving, still holding his hat in his hands, I scoldingly demanded, 'Go on. Go away. If you don't go, I will call my husband.'

"He slowly raised his head and looked at me and answered, 'Your husband's not at home.'

"It startled me, and I asked, 'How do you know he isn't at home?'

"In a very flat voice he replied, 'If he is home, it's because he's sick. He wouldn't stay home with you unless he was sick.' Then he turned around and very slowly walked away.

"I shut the door and leaned against it. I couldn't finish washing those dishes. After a while I went in and sat down and started thinking about how little my husband did stay at home. I wondered if the tramp was right and if God sent him to bring me to my senses. My thoughts went back over the morning. I had scolded my husband. I had not been kind to him the evening before. A thousand little ugly things raised their heads. I took a good look at myself, and I didn't like what I saw. That day I asked God to help me change my life and fill it full of good things, and today, like Paul, 'I count not myself to have apprehended; but. . .I press on."

Every person chooses his way of life. Maybe it would be more often true to say, "Everyone drifts into his way of life." Jesus called Himself "The Way," and His voice must have been very quiet and engaging when He said to those fishermen on the shores of Galilee, "Follow me. ' His voice comes down through the ages, "Follow me, and I will show you a better way of life." God never drives people into a better way. With all of His power, He uses no force to make anyone choose the high road. Every person's life is what he decides to let God make it.

Happiness, joy, and beauty are not something to be put on, but that which comes from within. Whatever is done on the outside must harmonize with the personality that is on the inside.

What a person is depends on his desire to be, his discernment of the open doors to truth, health and enlightenment, or whether he spends all his time in self-defense. New life and inner joy begin when any person starts thinking as himself and realizing the meaning of *to thine own self be true.*

It is very revealing when a person becomes aware of how he really feels and what he really thinks.

CHAPTER VIII

THINK FOR YOURSELF

The maxim, think for yourself, is basic; but the further maxim, think socially, must be added if philosophy is to do its whole duty.

— Edgar Sheffield Brightman

Those who have finished by making all others think with them, have usually been those who began by daring to think for themselves.

— Colton

EACH ONE IS TO THINK *FOR* HIMSELF.

Statistics reveal that *only 7 per cent of the people in the United States think for themselves.* Until one can think for himself, he is a nobody — drifting on an unidentified ocean. Each must have his own ideas or they will never become a part of him.

It is a part of being adult to understand that someone else may have a system of values very different from your own, and yet just as valid. At first this scares one when he realizes that his spiritual and moral codes must stand the tests of life. Too often people do not stop to examine why they believe as they do. They identify themselves with a system so unwittingly that to think in terms of another that works just as well almost questions one's own existence.

Jesus required of His disciples that each one must think for himself. That is why one must get the barriers from his eyes that prevent his seeing the needs of others and helping them.

There is no way that people can be in intellectual agreement on everything they think.

As one examines his values and ideas and convictions, and compares them with other people's, it will make his true values stronger and will help him to discard those that have no real worth.

When one is able to think for himself, he then realizes the essential point which Jesus was trying to emphasize — that he does not have to *like* the values of others, much less adopt them, but he must acknowledge that they exist, and that they have a right to exist. This can reinforce his own convictions through reason instead of blind belief. It is always better to hold a position from strength rather than weakness. Feeling threatened by faith or codes that differ only proclaims the shaky and shallow grasp of one's own principles.

An open mind and a thorough study of all beliefs is a fine avenue for a developed life and understanding. Thinking for oneself gives the opportunity of proper evaluation.

When one thinks for himself, he is able to have the best in himself and to know what is best for himself. Colleen Townsend Evans was, before her marriage, one of the most promising stars of Hollywood. When she goes back to Hollywood from her mission work, her friends often turn to her and say, "Colleen, isn't it a rather drab life that you are now living? Don't you miss the lights, the cameras, the publicity and seeing your name in big letters on the front of the theatre? After people were calling you the most beautiful starlet that Hollywood has seen, isn't it dull just talking to young people, reading the Bible to them and telling them about Christ?" And she simply says, "I just smile when they talk like that, and I say to them, 'Why, you don't know anything about living. I thought I was living when they called me so beautiful and so talented. I never knew anything about living until I gave my heart to Jesus Christ.'"

Babe Didrickson, the greatest woman athlete of the half century, was critically ill in Galveston, Texas. After her death her husband said, "Babe never prayed to win a golf tournament. She only prayed to live. She wanted to live at her best."

The modern business world has provided avenues for some men to become great. But others have been dwarfed by its demands, techniques and circumstances. The outcome depends more on the quality of the person than the quantity of the breaks.

Sydney Harris has compared this dilemma to that of the unborn child who has not received sufficient nourishment. Under these conditions he will draw strength from the tissues of his mother and practically destroy her. In the same way, man's drives, ambitions, and tactics can make him such a part of a machine, and so definitely materialistic, that they can eat the substance of the soul and destroy its opportunity to bring the true values of life.

Every person can see how another profession or personality is taking a toll of the whole person, but he is often very late in discovering what is happening to himself.

Hard working, successful men readily discern how the wastrel and ne'er-do-wells place pleasure and indolence above the whole personality. One has much difficulty, however, in perceiving how his ambition for gain and prominence is consuming his opportunities for the spirit.

Psychiatrists have shown through the history of their research how man must face the question of means and ends. Communists say that the end justifies the means. Also the perspective must be considered as to a proper end. The evolution of psychiatry is seen from Freud to Adler and then to Frankl. At first, Freud thought man's end was the will to pleasure. Adler saw the end as man's will to power. Frankl sees man's deepest will as the will to meaning.

To have a lesser end than to have meaning to his life robs man of thinking as himself — the person he is to be — and does, as Harris describes, "draws nourishment from the tissues of the soul and leaves it a wrinkled husk."

The unique meaning to every life is linked with the quality of man thinking for himself.

THE BASIC CAUSE OF MAN'S FAILURE TO LIVE AND TO THINK FOR HIMSELF IS FEAR.

Fear is an emotion that comes to every person in his efforts to live and survive. How one recognizes fear and resolves it determines his spiritual progress. One who tries to exist in a state of fear will destroy himself, and very quickly! It is this state of fear that Paul mentioned when he wrote: "God hath not given us the spirit of fear." Someone recently said that the two greatest enemies to a joyful life are *Fear of the Past* and *Fear of the Future*. The Fear of the Past centers around guilt. It did not have to be written in the Bible that "your sins will find you out" and that "With what measure ye mete it shall be measured to you again." This did not have to be written in the Bible for one to know that it is true. God left a witness of this great truth in the heart. How often men have said, "I deserve this and worse," or "I had it coming to me." Men without God live in constant fear of the past.

They likewise live in fear of the future. Uneasiness, fretfulness and worry are the close companions of people who have not anchored their lives in God. One of the glorious things about Jesus and Paul was that they were courageous. Quietly, with beautiful poise, they walked along the dangerous pathway of life with perfect assurance. When fears came they resolved them through the peace that God brings. They were anchored to the great rock-ribbed truth that *this is God's world.* "And we know that God works all things together for good to those that love Him, to those who are the called according to his purpose."

The natural reaction for people in fear is to try to control the fear or to run away from it. Fear is the emotion that is prominent in everyone. It has to be dealt with in a very severe manner — by admitting it, by facing it and by finding the way to resolve it.

Nouns which usually refer to fear in one of its shapes or forms, whether the user realizes it or not, are: anxiety, dismay, worry, apprehension, timidity, shyness, dread, fright, alarm, panic, terror and horror.

Old fears have been lived with so long that they rush back along the emotional grooves very quickly and easily. A sudden circumstance, an unusual situation, a word in a book or spoken by another, can touch off a terrifying descent of naked fear. It is better to endure the tension and the torment of longing to run away and escape than to lose self-respect and miss the opportunity to live.

Everyone needs to understand the basic factors in fear.

Fear is aroused by danger.

This danger can be to the individual, to someone he loves, to his possessions, his health, his peace of mind, his security, his ego, his liberty, his reputation, his character, his independence, his ideals, his beliefs, his virility, his sense of importance, or his self-esteem.

Since the purpose of fear is to insure survival, it will come to everyone. There is no way that a person can keep from experiencing the emotion of fear. Therefore, he needs to examine very closely the causes of his fear and learn how to resolve the fear in a wholesome manner. One should never try to deny his fears; rather, he should admit the fear and let God's Spirit and the right counsel lead him through it. God will lead through the valley of the shadow of fear. A recognition that guidance will come, in time for any action, takes away the anxiety that closes the door between the conscious and the unconscious. God's Spirit continually calls attention to the great *now,* always a new beginning, unfettered by the past, set free to be God's child. Response to this call brings constant renewal of life, which always has one on the edge of a new creation.

Fear is caused by the prospect of harm.

When anyone feels his peace of mind is going to be harmed he begins to fear. Harm to the physical body also arouses fear – this can be in the form of fear concerning automobile accidents, sickness, starvation, being bitten by a dog, snakes, burglars, falling.

Fear is caused more by other types of feelings.

These are fear of being disliked, fear of rejection, fear of ridicule, fear of being misunderstood, fear of hurt feelings, fear of disapproval, fear of sarcasm, fear of being bossed, fear of being imposed upon, fear of loneliness, fear of losing love, power, prestige, etc.

Among these fears the one that seems to be most prominent in the human personality is the danger of domination. Fear of this type is usually referred to as fear of loss of personality, that one's ego will not survive, that one's free will is then lost.

Another source of fear is the feeling of inadequacy. Such a person thinks he us unable to cope with things, so he is in constant fear of something turning up which he can not handle.

Facing up to the fact of these fears is the first step of dealing with them in a healthy and spiritual way. If one does not face his fears, then he remains in a state of fear and reaps the consequences of their destructive powers.

Fear and cowardice are not the same thing. Because of the failure to distinguish between fear and cowardice, all the scorn and disapproval of cowardice are commonly applied to fear as well. Children are brought up to be ashamed of both, without any difference being made between the two. The ideal of bravery and courage is considered identical with the ideal of fearlessness.

Fear does not prevent bravery; fright and courage go hand in hand, and the common belief that heroes are fearless is erroneous. The most daring acts of courage are by people who are not trying to prove something but who face fear and overcome it. Severe "stage fright" goes with most great artistic performances and with public speakers.

Cowardice is giving over to fears – bravery is overcoming the fears by acknowledging them and doing something about them.

There is only one power strong enough to destroy fear. Man cannot run away from fear. He can not control it. But man can turn his fear over to God and learn how "perfect love casts out all fear."

Mark Twain was known for cynical remarks about the church and religion. But there were times when he honestly revealed his feelings. One day the conversation in the barber shop centered around what could not be understood. Twain spoke up, "It is not what I don't understand in the Bible that brothers me. It is what I do understand." Every person needs to act upon the knowledge he does have. The longest trip begins with the first step.

Begin today the joy of thinking for yourself.

CHAPTER IX

THINK THROUGH YOURSELF

Living truth is that alone which has its origin in thinking. Just as a tree bears year after year the same fruit and yet fruit which is each year new, so must all permanently valuable ideas be continually born again in thought.

— *Albert Schweitzer*

EACH PERSON MUST THINK *THROUGH* HIMSELF.

In Enid Bagnold's searching play, "The Chinese Prime Minister," the leading character, who is seventy years old, says: "There is a me I have not conquered yet – or ever found." This alludes to a deeply significant fact – that there is a self beyond the knowledge that one has. And for all that one knows, there is another and another which must be satisfied if one is to live comfortably in his own skin. This is not an abstract philosophy, though one could carry it to that; it is actually a down to earth reality. It is the self in everyone that matters, that self that is beneath the surface – like an angry volcano that is ready to erupt – that asks of the right marriage, the house, the college education, the success of the children, the car, the clothes, the travel. "Is that all? Is this what life is all about?" Life is found in a movement, not in form or art including the art of living. Life is bringing order out of chaos, but the chaos has to be there as working substances or the order becomes flat, tasteless, hollow, barren.

When one gets to know himself, he must get on through self to God. Catherine Marshall has written a wonderful book, "BEYOND OURSELVES."

How does one achieve creative meaning? There is only one way. It is through commitment. One must do something, master something, and submit constantly to discipline and correction. This does not mean the only satisfaction is in a career. It means being committed to God – to where there is an interest in life, a cause, to where there is something in which one can involve himself to the highest and best.

When one comes to find the self beyond the self, he has found the secret door. It remains a secret because each one is individual. What holds the eyes from seeing it is that outer layer, the epidermis self. This self does not really want life; it wants death, or at least a somnolent state very close to it. Life means consciousness on many levels.

If one is to think through himself, it means more conflict, more pain, more unrest, more engagement and participation and paradox, not less. If one wishes to escape, he can; it is treacherously easy. If one chooses to pull an oar along with other fallible men and women, there is no promise except blisters and the formidable reward of being counted. This is the choice of life — *escape or commitment.* You must make a commitment. You cannot have both.

Everyone thinks through himself by being displeased with what he is. If one is satisfied with where he is, he can never keep growing.

When one thinks he has enough, he perishes.

The poet, Edgar A. Guest, has described how to think through self:

> I have to live with myself and so,
> I want to be fit for myself to know.
> I want to be able, as days go by,
> Always to look myself straight in the eye.
> I don't want to stand with the setting sun
> And hate myself for the things I've done.

The joy and meaning in life is in the process of going from one plateau of life to another. In this process man constantly goes through self to God. He then becomes aware of meaning and how the will to meaning holds possibilities for his freedom and enjoyment.

Viktor E. Frankl found his psychiatric approach — that the deepest desire in man is the will to meaning — by seeing humanity under its strongest tests of life. He discovered in a German concentration camp that only the ones who had a *will to meaning* survived. This outstanding physician has also seen the *will to pleasure* become a self-defeating principle. The more any person strives for pleasure, the less likely he is to gain it. Pleasure and happiness are always by-products of selfhood. The more one directly aims at pleasure, the more he misses it. Frankl also researched the will to power to its conclusion and says that it is a means to an end which can not hold ultimate satisfaction. The way to think through yourself lies in *the will to have meaning to your life*. Dr. Frankl makes a good illustration of the boomerang which everyone generally assumes to return to the thrower. Actually it returns when the thrower has missed his target. Similarly, man returns to himself, and thinks through himself, too concerned with the real person, only after he has missed his goal for life, only after he has failed to find meaning in his way of life and in life.

This meaning is discovered as man commits himself to One who is greater than himself — this One is God. The meaning which man is to fulfill is something beyond himself, never just himself. Only if this meaning maintains this otherness beyond self can it exert upon anyone that quality of motivation, inspiration, and imperativeness which yields to an accurate analysis of self. Meaning must not coincide with being. It must be ahead of being. Meaning sets the pace for being. Existence will falter if it is not lived in terms of transcendence, in terms of something beyond self.

Herein is seen the difference between a pacemaker and an appeasing kind of peacemaker. Pacemakers confront humanity with meanings and values and thereby enable the opportunity for a meaningful orientation. The appeasing peacemaker (peace at any price) alleviates the burden of meaning confrontation. Moses is understood in this sense as a pacemaker. He did not soothe man's conscience but stirred it up. When Moses presented the Ten Commandments, he did not spare his people with a confrontation with ideals and values.

This appeasing peacemaker does not persist to win the fight within and emerge from his cocoon. He remains a worm crawling in the dust. He tries to reconcile others with himself. Let's face facts, he states. Why should anyone worry about his shortcomings? There are only a few who live up to ideals. Try to find peace of mind, quietness of soul, and keep from upsetting people. Don't get involved in these concepts, situations, lives, and persons outside self that stir up the human personality. This kind of peacemaker forgets the lessons of history and the warnings that God has revealed to man. Take man as he is and he becomes worse. Take him as he ought to be and he can be helped to become that person.

Man, then, is not only responsible for the fulfillment of the specific meaning of his own life, but he is also responsible to something, be it society, humanity, conscience, cause, or as he does come eventually to know — to God.

Frankl, in presenting his logotherapy, does not permit the possibility of error as any reason to not obey the inner conscience. Existence involves the risk of error. A world in which man may become a fiend or a saint is preferable to a totally conformist, collectivist world.

Thinking through himself cleanses man from the hidden debris he has never faced. Often in this debris he feels life has handed him a lemon. What can man do with a lemon?

Dale Carnegie, in his book HOW TO STOP WORRYING AND START LIVING, tells about dropping in one day at the University of Chicago and asking the Chancellor, Robert Maynard Hutchins, how he kept from worrying. The Chancellor replied, "I have always tried to follow a bit of advice given to me by the late Julius Rosenwald, President of Sears, Roebuck and Company, 'When you have a lemon, make a lemonade.'"

Then Carnegie gave two splendid illustrations. He said, "Here is an interesting and stimulating story of a woman I know who did just that. Her name is Thelma Thompson, and she lives at 100 Morningside Drive, New York City. 'During the war,' she said, as she told me of her experience, 'during the war, my husband was stationed at an Army training camp near the Mojave Desert, in California. I went to live there in order to be near him. I hated that place. I loathed it. I had never before been so miserable. My husband was ordered out on maneuvers in the Mojave Desert, and I was left in a tiny shack alone. The heat was unbearable — 125 degrees in the shade of a cactus. Not a person to talk to but Mexicans and Indians, and they couldn't speak English. The wind blew incessantly, and all the food I ate, and the very air I breathed, were filled with sand, sand, sand!

"'I was so utterly wretched, so sorry for myself, that I wrote to my parents. I told them I was giving up and coming home. I said I couldn't stand it one minute longer. I would rather be in jail! My father answered my letter with just two lines — two lines that will always sing in my memory — two lines that completely altered my life:

Two men looked out from prison bars,
One saw the mud, the other saw the stars.

"'I read those two lines over and over. I was ashamed of myself. I made up my mind I would find out what was good in my present situation; I would look for the stars.

"'I made friends with the natives, and their reaction amazed me. When I showed interest in their weaving and pottery, they gave me presents of their favorite pieces which they had refused to sell to tourists. I studied the fascinating forms of the cactus and the yucca and the Joshua trees. I learned about prairie dogs, watched for the desert sunsets, and hunted for seashells that had been left there millions of years ago.

"'What brought about this astonishing change in me? The Mojave Desert hadn't changed. The Indians hadn't changed. But I had. I had changed my attitude of mind. And by doing so, I transformed a wretched experience into the most exciting adventure of my life. I was stimulated and excited by this new world that I had discovered. I was so excited I wrote a book about it — a novel that was published under the title *Bright Ramparts*. . .I had looked out of my self-created prison and found the stars.' Life handed her a lemon so she made a lemonade."

The second illustration read: "I once visited a happy farmer down in Florida who turned even a poison lemon into a lemonade. When he first got this farm, he was discouraged. The land was so wretched he could neither grow fruit nor raise pigs. Nothing thrived but scrub oaks and rattlesnakes. Then he got his idea. He would turn his liability into an asset; he would make the most of those rattlesnakes. To everyone's amazement, he started canning rattlesnake meat. When I stopped to visit him a few years ago, I found that tourists were pouring in to see his rattlesnake farm at the rate of twenty thousand a year. His business was thriving. I saw poison from the fangs of his rattlers being shipped to laboratories to make anti-venom toxin; I saw rattlesnake skins being sold at fancy prices to make women's shoes and handbags. I saw canned rattlesnake meat being shipped to customers all over the world. I bought a picture postcard of the place and mailed it at the local post office of the village, which had been rechristened 'Rattlesnake, Florida,' in honor of a man who had turned a poison lemon into sweet lemonade."

Don't ever stop with the realization that you are a lemon. Think on through until the lemon becomes lemonade.

CHAPTER X

THINK OF YOURSELF

Thinkers are scarce as gold; but he, whose thoughts embrace all their subjects, who pursues it uninterruptedly and fearless of consequences, is a diamond of enormous size.

— Lavater

Change your way of thinking of yourself and you will change your way of life from one level of joy to another higher level each day.

EVERY PERSON MUST THINK *OF* HIMSELF.

Everyone must ask whether he really wants himself, or would he like to exchange that self for some other he fancies prettier or richer or more gifted or more fortunate or more loved. Many people are privately convinced that they are singled out for trouble, that they have it just a little harder than others. It is not so, and it is one of the most dangerous of delusions. It fritters away the energies that should go directly into the self that each one now is. For a person to continue in this vein, he is guilty of what Dr. Edward Teller, the noted physicist, called "unused excellencies," which he said lie dormant in almost everyone. The continuing challenge to everyone is to want self — his own self, not somebody else's.

EACH CAN WORK WITH WHAT HE IS. HE CAN ONLY WORK WITH WHAT HE IS. Beware of taking courses which in some way seek to get people to be someone else other than the true self. A self is not additive; it is expansive. Every ounce of skill, every scrap of learning contributing toward expansion is worthwhile. The goal is to release the self inside, not to create it. If life seems empty and unrewarding, perhaps one is not thinking enough of himself. Unless one really wants himself, he cannot expect other people to want that self.

Billy Sunday used to tell young people that if they could do the job as well as a thousand others, they would have a thousand competitors. However, if they could do the job better than the thousand, they would not have to seek the job, the job would seek them.

When one is true to himself, there is no competition with anyone else. People in God's will are not in competition with anyone.

As one thinks of himself, he must always desire to put more into life than he gets out of it. One does not turn to the world because it owes him a living, but because he owes the world something.

Former President John F. Kennedy's statement: "Do not ask what your country can do for you, but what you can do for your country," will always be a challenge.

IF YOU DO NOT PERSIST IN SEEING TO IT THAT YOUR LIFE BECOMES SOMETHING, YOU CAN BE RATHER CERTAIN THAT NO ONE ELSE WILL.

In this particular setting consideration needs to be given to what you are going to do with your life, or what is left of your life.

Buell G. Gallagher has drawn a rather drastic picture of the college rebel. He states that the tragedy of today's college rebel is that he has no bona fide tragedy of his own and that he has no willingness to learn about the subject from older generations. Gallagher believes that this fact has a drastic side effect on this particular group, for without tragedy there can be no compelling hope — no Utopia. Having nothing to die for, one has little to live for. He points out that historically, hope, as distinguished from mere optimism, has been the child of despair, sired by tragedy. His illustration of this is that Plato, emerging with a dream of the Republic, contemplated the ruins of his beloved Athens.

To think of yourself, you must ask what I am doing to myself. After all you are the only one who can do any permanent damage to yourself. Many people will not permit themselves to be healthy, happy and useful. Everyone must face up to the fact that he is taking joy, the fun, out of living by his own attitude toward himself.

Are you taking the real joy and the fun of living out of your life?

This appears ridiculous. It would seem that anyone would let himself or herself be happy. But this is not true. There are many people who constantly inflict punishment on themselves because they feel they are not worthy of happiness and will in no way permit sunlight, love and understanding to enter their lives. They seem to think of additional ways each day to submerge every new day into gloom and despair. Also, they destroy every head that comes on the horizon to brighten their day. Self-destruction in psychological terms is masochism. The way that this pattern of behaviour can be changed is to change the image of self and begin to believe that God has something better than what is now being experienced.

A French writer in the 1930's said: "Our generation won't go to the moon. The next generation will talk about it, but they will not go. The reason is that we don't believe we can."

Isn't this the handicap that every person faces? The beginning for everything is the willingness to believe – to have faith – to think with expectancy.

I. B. M. has a theme for all their employees – "To think is to achieve."

Milton emphasized the importance of what one believes in regard to his thinking by writing:

"The mind is its own place, and in itself
Can make a Heaven of Hell, a Hell of Heaven."

Gilbert Chesterton had a discerning philosophy in this regard. He proclaimed: "Tell me what a man thinks about God and I will tell you what he thinks about the sum total of life."

Abraham Lincoln often spoke of different aspects of his faith. One of his observations was: "I accept what I can of the Bible by reason. When my reason can not comprehend it, I go by faith until my reason catches up with my faith."

This is the way that all people learn to comprehend and appropriate the gifts of God. Everyone is constantly placed in situations and circumstances where there is no direction for him to take. When these arise, it is through the avenue of faith that one functions and keeps on until insight catches up with him; then it is that faith gives over to sight. Any time there is sight, one is not operating by faith. Faith, then, is to take man into new ventures, places and knowledge until reason and insight can begin to take their part in human discernment and understanding.

The faith, spirit, and attitude toward God and life enable one to make the impossible situation a joy. One can hardly imagine anyone thinking of the Cross as joy, but Jesus did.

There are many types of faith which man uses in life.

One drives a car with faith that the mechanical devices will continue to be safe and that his tires will hold out in the manner which those who made them have said.

People go to work with the faith that their employer will fulfill his part of their contract by seeing that there is something to be done and that the pay he has promised will be given.

Friends carry on their personal relationships with faith that the enjoyment and happiness that they have shared will continue to bring satisfactory and delightful times in the future.

Faith in God is different from these types of faith, but it is related to every relationship of life. Faith is in the present tense; yet it is also in the active voice. Remind yourself constantly: "God works all things together for good to those who love Him and are then called according to His purpose."

Many people try to oversimplify this passage of Scripture by saying that all things work together for good; therefore, whatever things happen are good. What a terrible interpretation. It binds some people with emotional frustration and often much heartache.

The outstanding and great woman Mabel Starnes said of those who came in and told her she should be thankful for her broken back that she would have exploded if just one more person had told her that. A broken back is not good. It is painful and terrible.

Try to tell some brokenhearted husband, "You are so fortunate that your wife has died." He is grieving and you are saying "rejoice." Grief is the result of love.

All such conversation is ridiculous.

Another false interpretation of this verse is to tell those in trials, tribulation, and trouble: "Smile through your trial, your tribulation, or your trouble – smile – you are on God's Candid Camera."

But the faith that God reveals to His disciples is to accept the tragedies of life as tragedies, but to remember that God will lead you through the avenue of faith to have strength in your desperation and despair and will eventually lead you to have the power to live and survive. Most of the time you will feel that you are walking in the valley because this is the habitat of man, but there are occasionally mountains of sunlight and understanding to show the way and mark the trail.

Life can take on new proportions when one quits making himself or herself miserable, and lets faith, love and joy flow.

Everything that has happened in your life has the seed for a greater benefit. What you accept and believe is the basis for what you will achieve. Think of yourself – no one else can.

CHAPTER XI

THINK BY YOURSELF

They are never alone who are accompanied by noble thoughts.

— Sir P. Sidney

There are times in everyone's life when necessity demands that he withdraw from the influence and hypnotism of others to think by himself and find himself.

EVERY PERSON MUST THINK *BY* HIMSELF.

If one is to appreciate himself and enjoy himself, he must do what is required in knowing another person. He must spend time with himself, be alone sometimes and be silent, retreat from the pattern and habit without, and cultivate what is within.

There are four kinds of alones and each is needful, though some are more readily attained than others.

One is to be alone at home, in familiar surroundings, but without demands, without turning to the radio or television to keep him company. But how he is to do this is up to the individual.

Clara Barton was asked on one occasion, "How was it that you could do nursing when you hadn't had any experience and you were not used to suffering and seeing blood?" And she replied, "By utterly forgetting myself."

It is through being alone that one gathers strength to overcome handicaps and circumstances. Carrie Jacobs Bond was left as an invalid with an enormous debt when her husband died. She tried to paint china and sell it, but nobody seemed to want it. Then she wrote songs, but the publishers didn't want them. And then, over her circumstances, she gave to the world those beautiful songs: "A Perfect Day," "I Love You Truly," and "Just A-Wearying For You." Carrie Jacobs Bond stated, "I learned to conquer my handicaps."

A second kind of aloneness is at large. In this a person goes to a museum or art gallery or concert or play or film or restaurant or just for a walk along busy streets alone. As he goes along he might react to the painting or performance or street sounds and sights inside his own head without trying to communicate it. He should absorb, listen, look, digest, and reflect.

Each individual must sum up at night what he has done by day, and in the morning what must be done. Dress and undress the soul; mark the decay or the growth of it.

There is also a traveling alone — whether it is on a plane, a ship, or just a city bus — in a foreign country or only a different section of his own town or city. Being alone in an alien situation is instructive. Sometimes there is a certain amount of panic, but one is not to be surprised.

There is an intense aloneness of living for a time — hours or days or weeks — on a sand dune or in a forest or on an ice flow — alone with the components of the universe, perhaps with God. This is, of course, the most drastic, the most powerful kind of aloneness. Few can do it often, and many do not want to. But nobody who has ever really tried it is ever quite so alone again — he has met himself. And, through meeting himself, he has come to know God in a different and better way.

Helen Keller, at the well in Alabama, where the first word — water — flashed through to her — and then the concept of God — said, "I thank God for my handicaps, for through my handicaps, I've found my life, my work, and my God."

A popular song expresses it in the words of the young: "I was like a clock, without a tock; But now I'm glad I'm living, 'cause I know what makes me tick."

The person who learns to think by himself also realizes the necessity of taking one day at a time. Multitudes of ideas, problems, tasks and even failures try to capture your attention. But you can not afford to overtax your mind, body and spirit by taking on more than one day at a time.

No one can live in the past nor in the future. Everyone must live in the present — by living one day at a time and making it what it should be. The only thing about the past is to find forgiveness and to learn. As to the future, prepare for it today.

The meaningful life is basically sharing from the overflow of the heart and mind what God has done for that person. This became personal when an outstanding heart specialist gave me a little book that stopped me from too much concern about tomorrow and inspired me to begin living one day at a time. The book is entitled, *A Way of Life*. It was written by a very great medical doctor, William Osler. Many people say that they would like to be different persons — they want to have meaning to life. Then they add, "I don't know what to do or how to find it."

Man's biggest problem is how to live with himself. Since man is spiritual he needs to have meaning to life; a reason for living. Because he is finite everything he seeks is threatened. This dual nature results in anxiety. Man may try to overcome this anxiety by drifting into sensuality, but more often he asserts himself in pride at the expense of others. Man rebels against his own humanity by refusing to accept his limitations and by claiming for himself that which belongs to God alone. He finds himself in the peculiar position of having his frustrations and unhealthy emotions arise from the same source as his creativity and nobility. Only when man realizes that it does not detract from his dignity to recognize that he is esentially the same as others can he begin to face his emotional, spiritual and mental maturity. When he accepts the fact that he is a part of the human race he can begin to realize the purpose of his existence. However we may try, there is no way to avoid the uncomfortable reality of being human, and until we know what that means, we will know little else.

This starts by learning today what you can — by doing today what you can — then tomorrow's life will be what it needs to be. In a sense, man lives only as he begins to realize the human mystery — who he is, his basic instincts, how to overcome his inadequacies, and how to patiently do this one day at a time. Humanity's peril, in the face of great opportunities of the spirit, is that people may choose not to live — at least not deeply or greatly. This is man's scandal and also his opportunity for glory.

He can choose to be what he wants to be.

The basic teaching of Jesus is to live one day at a time. By choosing the best today, tomorrow you will be prepared for the right. He said, "Take therefore no thought for tomorrow for the morrow shall take thought for the things of itself. Sufficient unto the day is the evil thereof."

Both worry and peace come, not from circumstances, but from the heart.

Alistair MacLean quotes a story from Tauler, the German mystic. One day Tauler met a beggar. "God give you a good day, my friend," he said. The beggar answered, "I thank God I never had a bad one." Then Tauler said, "God give you a happy life, my friend." "I thank God," said the beggar, "I am never unhappy." Tauler in amazement said, "What do you mean?" "Well," said the beggar, "when it is fine, I thank God; when it rains, I thank God; when I have plenty, I thank God; when I am hungry, I thank God; and since God's will is my will, and whatever pleases Him pleases me, why should I say I am unhappy when I am not?" Tauler looked at the man in astonishment. "Who are you?" he asked. "I am a king," said the beggar. "Where then is your kingdom?" asked Tauler. And the beggar answered quietly: *"In my heart."*

Often it is said that people want love and understanding; actually they want to express the deepest love of their life to someone. The only way this can be done is to do something today of the deepest fulfillment of life. Only by doing the best today can a dream be realized. Don't delay. "Now is the accepted time; now is the day of salvation." Doing the best you can today develops maturity and sound thinking for tomorrow. A religion for today demands that life be faced as it comes, and not evaded. The future is today. There is no tomorrow.

Among the ways in which people seek to adjust to life, let us consider the following:

THE FOOLISH WAY

This person puts the blame on things themselves. He goes on all his life thinking that if only he tried another woman, or went for a more expensive vacation, or whatever, then, this time, he really would catch the mysterious something we are all after.

He looks at the horizon, the falsehoods, the frauds, the quackeries that have caused men to be discontented rather than at the truth and happiness that tumble at his feet.

THE FADED WAY

This person decides that life is a fading dream. He says that only the young should dream. He settles down and learns not to expect too much and represses his deepest desires as unattainable. Even though this is a better way than the first, and makes people much happier, it leaves out the real zest for living, the real power for attainment, and the fact of infinite happiness. He no longer has incentive for living and has given up in the battle.

THE FAITH WAY

The Christian discerns that people are not born with desires unless satisfaction for those desires exists. A duckling wants to swim; there is such a thing as water. A calf is hungry; the cow's milk meets his need. The human being longs for companionship; the loved ones respond.

Since man finds in himself a desire which no experience can satisfy, the probable explanation is that he was made for another world.

Earthly pleasures were never made to satisfy, but only to arouse, to suggest the real thing. One must never despise or be unthankful for the earthly blessings, but also one must never mistake for the real thing that which can only be a copy, an echo, a mirage.

A religion for today holds before its follower the wonderful opportunity of being in a right relationship with God and of having fulfilled in his life the deepest spiritual desires of the heart.

Carlyle once said: "Our main business is not to see what lies dimly at a distance, but to do what lies clearly at hand."

William Osler summarizes his philosophy of life in these lines from the Sanscrit:

> "Listen to the Exortation of the Dawn!
> Look to this Day!
> For it is Life, the very Life of Life.

In its brief Course lie all the
Varieties and Realities of your Existence:
The Bliss of Growth,
The Glory of Action,
The Splendour of Beauty;
For Yesterday is but a Dream
And Tomorrow is only a Vision;
But Today well lived makes
Every Yesterday a Dream of Happiness,
And every Tomorrow a Vision of Hope.
Look well therefore to this Day!
Such is the Salutation of the Dawn!"

God will bring meaning for today and this prepares each person for all the tomorrows and rids him from all the bondage of the past. This man must believe and receive.

A VERY TIMELY PRAYER

"Slow me down, Lord! Ease the pounding of my heart by the quieting of my mind. Steady my hurried pace with a vision of the eternal reach of Time, Give me, admist the confusion of my day, the calmness of the everlasting hills. Break the tension of my nerves and muscles with the soothing music of the singing streams that live in my memory. Help me to know the magical restorative power of sleep. Teach me the art of taking Minute Vacations. . .of slowing down to look at a flower, to chat with a friend, to pat a dog, to read a few lines from a good book.

Remind me each day of the Fable of the hare and the tortoise, that I may know that the race is not always to the swift; that there is more to life than increasing its speed. Let me look upward into the branches of the towering oak, and know that it grew because it grew slowly and well. Slow me down, Lord, and inspire me to send my roots deep into the soil of life's enduring values, that I may grow toward the stars of my greater destiny. Amen.

Thinking by yourself enables you to find the way within your own life. This is the only avenue for any quality to be truly yours.

It's your life you are betting. Make your bet! Be sure the stakes are what you want.

Thoughts To Consider

1. Think as yourself and begin to feel alive. The negative attitudes that come from playing a role in life are displaced by positive attitudes, inner joy and peace.

2. Think as yourself and find your place in life — what you are to do and what you can be.

3. Never let negative thinking remain in your mind. Replace it with the positive.

4. Think for yourself and by this overcome daily the fears that keep you from being yourself.

5. Think for yourself and the deepest desires begin to be yours.

6. Man does not act by reason alone, but by what he wants to do.

7. Great powers for healthy and meaningful living come through thinking for yourself.

8. Commitment opens the way to the self beyond self.

9. Think through yourself and be clean from the hidden debris that you have never faced.

10. The risk of error is much better than being a conformist or being an aid to a collective world.

11. If you do not persist in seeing that your life becomes something, you can be certain that no one else will.

12. Think of yourself as having significant meaning to God and to society.

13. God is always a good God. Believe this with all your heart and mind.

14. Think of yourself as you truly want to be.

15. Think of yourself — no one else can.

16. Think by yourself and receive the benefit of knowing yourself through the same procedure by which you would become acquainted with another person.

PART III

THE COURAGE TO BE YOURSELF

A coward flees backward, away from new things. A man of courage flees forward, in the midst of new things.

— Jacques Maritain

Courage is, on all hands, considered as an essential of high character.

— Froude

CHAPTER XII

COURAGE IS THE FIRST OF HUMAN QUALITIES

True courage is not the brutal force of vulgar heroes, but the firm resolve of virtue and reason.

— Paul Whitehead

Courage from hearts and not from number grows.

— Dryden

This is the age when everyone seems to think that all the inner conflicts of life can be changed by a pill. They can, if that certain pill happens to be courage. Doctors face patients every day who have gotten the idea that there is a magic in the physician's hands to make life take on new meaning, bring financial success, right marital relations, develop a strong ego, and create peace of heart. Men of medicine, as a rule, try to discourage such false notions, but the same people come the next day looking for a magical cure – only to be told that they must have the courage to be themselves and find the inner resources for a healthy life.

The secret to your life is found in the courage to be yourself and to concentrate your energies on that goal. "Courage," according to Tillich, "is self-affirmation 'in spite of', and the courage to be as oneself is self-affirmation of the self as itself. Self, cut off from participation in its world, is an empty shell, a mere possibility. It must act because it lives, but it must redo every action because acting involves him who acts in that upon which he acts. It gives content and for this reason it restricts his freedom to make of himself what he wants."

Winston Churchill has said that courage is the first of human qualities, because it is the only quality which guarantees all the others. Courage, in a certain sense, is brought about through spiritual self-suggestion, as it follows the guide of the inner conscience.

Since no man has courage, his means of attaining it is through desire. Whatever man becomes is rooted in his will to be courageous, to move beyond where he is, what he is, and beyond self. Man is called to have the courage to be. He answers. He is challenged. He obeys. In obeying, the will matures. As he matures in choosing – responding – desiring, courage grows.

In man's feeling for security, he is prone to stay in a safe structure. When he does this, he can never be courageous. *Safe structures destroy the inner man.* It is in learning to go from one structure to the other that progress is made. Jesus taught that man must risk his life if he ever finds it.

Dr. Connant, as a university president, had the picture of a turtle on his office wall. Underneath were these words, "The turtle does not make progress until he sticks out his neck."

When man's concern is for his neck, he cannot keep his eyes and goals on inner progress.

In this world, which is so tricky and baffling, it is an absolute necessity to measure the truth and consequence of every impulse. It is very easy to be more concerned about what you are going to get than what you are going to give. This predicament led the famed Peter Marshall to say, "It is the donation to life, not the duration of life that counts." *It is not how long one lives but how well one lives.*

President Calvin Coolidge was pinning a medal on a young man and praising him for his heroism. "Young man, this world doesn't remember individuals who are always getting. The world remembers individuals who are always giving out and doing good in the world," was his quiet but firm admonition.

Probably the fault for man's failures lies more in one fallacy than any other. It is the concept that he can get something for nothing. Too many people want a society free of murder, rape, robbery, riots, thievery, poverty, war and ghettos, but they are not willing to pay the price.

King David was offered a piece of land for nothing, but he was too wise to accept it. He replied,

" – I will surely buy it of you at a price; neither will I offer burnt offering unto the Lord my God of that which doth cost me nothing."

He was aware that real character comes as a result of a

tremendous price. Courage comes by believing your life is worth fighting for with everything you have.

Conscience is man's inner guide for what he is to do. Courage enables man to be true to his conscience. There are times when silence is golden; then there are times when silence is yellow.

Conscience is the simplest and clearest expression of the exalted character and dignity of human life.

Conscience is that faculty in man which attaches itself to the highest that he knows and tells him what the highest he knows demands that he do. It is the eye of the soul which looks out either towards God or towards what it regards as the highest, and therefore conscience records differently in different people. If one is in the habit of steadily facing himself with God, his conscience will always introduce God's perfect law and indicate what he should do. The point is, will he obey?

As Paul was writing to the Romans he reminded them that every man had something to guide him as to what God would have him to do. The Jews had been given the Law that was to show the direction in which God would have man move in his personal relationship to God; and to the Gentile, who had not had the privilege of studying the Bible, God had spoken through his conscience. Paul stated that "their conscience bore witness" of what God would have man to do.

Even though the expression "conscience" is not found in the Old Testament, the thought is usually expressed in statements concerning the heart. A good example concerns David: "And it came to pass afterward, that David's heart smote him, because he had cut off Saul's skirt." The expression "conscience" is derived etymologically from the Latin verb "to know with." It means a knowing together with something or someone.

This inner voice keeps reminding everyone of the evil that must be renounced and the good to be done. There is no grave deep enough to permanently bury evil. It must have its resurrection. The man who has done wrong has a serpent hibernating in his heart. For months, for years, it will show no sign of life; but one day it will lift its head and strike. The evil deed has been hidden, the sin buried, for years; but suddenly it will have a fearful resurrection. "Angels hear the throb of the heart and God counts the thoughts of the mind." The smallest trifle will suffice to call the sin out of its grave — the stirring of a leaf, the murmur of water, the sound of a voice, the sight of a face, the pronunciation of a name or a number — and lo! the graves are opened and the ghosts of man's former transgressions come forth to accuse him to his face! In that great description of conscience, "Toilers of the Sea," Victor Hugo says:

> "You can no more keep thought from returning to past transgression than keep the sea from returning to the shore after it has gone out. In the sea we call it the tide; but the guilty man calls it conscience. Conscience heaves the soul as the tide does the ocean."

Man's greatest victories are brought about by obedience to this conscience.

Paul told Timothy, "Now the end of the commandment is love out of a pure heart, and of a good conscience, and of faith unfeigned."

There are no blessings in life that can come except through having a good conscience.

Conscience is quite different from instinct. Instinct tells an animal what to do in order to preserve its own life, as well as that of its species. In wild animals the instinctive faculty works with perfect normalcy. Conscience, however, is an inner compelling urge of a holy, superhuman law which enables man to know right and to choose the way of life which he wants.

Conscience expresses itself sometimes before, sometimes during, and sometimes after the act involved. Before the act, it encourages one to carry out the act or advises one not to do it. During the act, the voice of the conscience is the weakest. It is most difficult for conscience to gain a hearing. After the act, the conscience usually speaks most strongly, either approving the deed and expressing satisfaction, or protesting against it and producing inner unrest and anxiety.

A GOOD CONSCIENCE BRINGS JOY AND UNDERSTANDING.

The feeling of pleasure and happiness which results from a good conscience surpasses all other feelings.

Courage enables you to find your way to follow the inner conscience and enjoy yourself.

CHAPTER XIII

COURAGE IS THE FAITH TO ACT

Courage that grows from constitution, often forsakes a man when he has occasion for it; courage which arises from a sense of duty, acts in a uniform manner.

— Addison

To see what is right and not to do it, is want of courage.

— Confucius

The courage to be yourself implies the courage to replace the old with the new. *In the new, there will be no old emotional patterns of behavior to rely on to make you feel secure.* The new is a risk and can not be calculated. It is the process of faith which waits, experiences and sees.

The joy and understanding which man desires is beyond mere existence. Life must have more than just a desire to keep alive. The biggest cowards and the most miserable people in the world are those who try to save their lives rather than give them to God and do His will.

"A man must live," the world said to Daniel when he read the proclamation of the king, Darius, that for thirty days no prayer should be offered save to Darius himself. "You need not pray at the open window where your enemies will see you; you can say your prayers, Daniel, in your secret chamber. Thus you will escape the lion's den." Such was the worldly counsel.

But Daniel said, "The man of faith and prayer must live within me"; and three times, as his custom was, Daniel opened his window toward Jerusalem and knelt down and prayed to the God of Abraham, Isaac and Jacob. They put him in a lion's den, but Daniel thought it was better to be in a lion's den with God than to have the wealth and approval of the king.

"A man must live," the world said to John Bunyan when he was arrested under Charles II. If John Bunyan had signed a paper saying he would not preach in public he could have escaped prison; and if at any time during his twelve years' imprisonment he had been willing to say that, he would have been released.

"A man must live," the world said to Bunyan, "especially a man with a dependent wife and little children, and particularly when one of those children is blind, like your poor girl, Mary." In the dungeon, Bunyan thought of that. He said that his heart was like to break when he thought of his poor family, and especially when he thought of his poor blind girl. "Oh, my poor blind one," he would say to himself, "what sorrows thou art likely to have in this

Every achievement and quality value in life comes as a result of faith. There are always presuppositions to any endeavor. For one to begin a life of being himself, he must believe that the real life in which God intends him to be is much more significant than any life which he can create for himself. He must believe there is a purpose for life and that he has a place to fill in life. Faith opens the way to live in harmony with the inner conscience. Where man hesitates, faith leads on.

Jesus stated: "All things are possible to him who believes."

You may be reading these lines after a period of great reverses; — life seems to have tumbled in — or you may have the world by the tail, swinging it around your head to do with as you please. Whatever emotional plane you are on, you have great powers never yet realized. Whether you admit it or not depends upon your capacity to face reality — you do have a low estimate of yourself; everybody does. And the quicker you join the human race, and admit your low esteem, the better for you.

Most people content themselves with constant complaining about their situations, circumstances, hard luck, and ill treatment. They would be much happier to realize they can have a new lease on life. Joy can replace sorrow; success can overcome failure; confidence can overpower timidity; and an interesting life can emerge from your boredom. But you must have faith that there is such an avenue for you or you will never start.

If you are not careful, you will adapt yourself to be a recipient of unhealthy emotions and unfortunate behavior patterns in an apathetic attitude toward your potentialities.

Raimundo De Ovies tells a story about a man who was able to buy the only book left from the great library of Alexandria, Egypt, when it burned. It contained information concerning the secret of "Touchstone." This was a small pebble that could change any common metal into pure gold. It was on the shores of the Black Sea, lying with thousands of other stones which looked exactly as it did. The real one would feel warm — the others would be cold.

He decided to throw the cold stones into the sea so that he would not pick up the same ones again. He gave three years to this pattern of action. Then one day he found a warm stone, but before he could stop himself he had thrown away the one thing he desired.

It is unfortunate that this generation has discarded a wonderful foundation for life — faith.

People have relegated faith to "belief in something unbelievable." Some theologians have defined faith as the state of being grasped by the power of being itself. The courage to be your authentic self is an expression of faith, and the meaning of faith must be understood through your courage to be that self. Faith is the experience of the power of courage.

Faith lies in the willingness and daring to believe that you were created to be somebody. It is belief that God, self-understanding, and courage to be will enable you to go through the painful process of being that person.

Faith enables you to identify. *There are two great needs for everyone. One is to identify with someone greater than he is — the second is to find his own personhood.* At this time consider your identification with God in Christ. The relation of the base of your being is often expressed in symbols so that you may have a picture of what is taking place. You find yourself participating as a part of society, groups in society, and also as an individual standing alone. The way you relate these two parts of your being will determine the special character of your courage to be. If you accept both, one part of your being can result from mystical experiences. All mystics draw their power for the courage to be from the divine substance through which they experience union or *at-one-ment*.

Such mystical identification transcends the heroic and i self-sacrifice. It is self-surrender in a higher, more comp more meaningful form. *The difference in the immature mature is that the immature are anxiously wanting to d for a cause. The mature are willing to live humbly for one.*

Faith, as a state of being, enables you to constantl beyond your past and present state to be yourself.

The mystic affirms his essential self in identifications power of Christ and can say with Paul, "It is not I, but Ch lives in me." He is able to move from one structure to without the anxieties of fear, death, fate and despair everything that is participates in the power of being, the of identity on which mysticism is based cannot be abser any form of religious experience.

Individualization as the other pole, expresses itself in a p encounter with God. The courage gained from a p relationship with God is the courage to have confidence personal reality manifested in religious experience. Faith road for both mystical experiences and personal confi Martin Luther sought for a person-to-person encounter with In him the courage of confidence reached its highest point history of Christian thought. His writings show Luther's c "in spite of." He moved through his terrible difficulties i power of courage derived from his strong confidence in Go his personal relationship with God.

Faith goes beyond the mystical experience and the h encounter with God. There are times when the my experience seems to be nearer to absolute faith, but this is no case. There is an aspect of skepticism in faith which is not f in the mystical experience. Mysticism is able to go beyon specific contents and use them as stepping-stones. Meaningless on the other hand, as seen in skepticism, denies the con without making any use of it. Courage is more radical and beyond mysticism.

life! How thou must go naked and hungry and beg on the streets and be beaten and starved; and now I cannot so much as endure the thought that the winds should blow upon thee!" Yes, a man must live, and a man's family must live; but John Bunyan remained in the dungeon and gave over his concerns, blind Mary and all, to the keeping of God. Toward the end of his imprisonment he wrote that glorious passage in which he said, "Unless I am willing to make of my conscience a continual slaughter shop and butchery; unless I am willing to pluck out my eyes and let the blind lead me, then God Almighty being my witness and my defense — if it shall please him to let frail life last that long — the moss shall grow upon these eyebrows before I surrender my principles or violate my conscience."

Courage is the faith to act upon the inner light and to move through the valley where you are to where you are to be.

CHAPTER XIV

COURAGE IS THE POWER TO FORGIVE

Courage consists not in hazarding without fear, but being resolutely minded in a just cause.

— Plutarch

To err is human; to forgive, divine.

— Pope

Never does the human soul appear so strong and noble as when it foregoes revenge and dares to forgive an injury.

— E. H. Chapin

Along with faith you must be willing to accept the forgiveness of God, forgive other people, and forgive yourself. Sometimes the forgiveness of self is the most difficult, as man fights in his rebellion to his own humanity. But always remember: God does not keep reminding you of your past. He keeps reminding you of what you can be.

When realization comes about the role you have played concerning self and what you have made of yourself, you come to some phases of hysteria, despair and destructiveness that make progress difficult. When you have a tremendous problem in accepting God's forgiveness and forgiving yourself, realize that this relates to the low esteem you have of yourself and your sense of unworthiness. Whether you are worthy of forgiveness is not for you to decide. God decided this in the death of Jesus on a cross. It is yours to accept for your own good, for what God can make out of you, and for what God can do through you for others. Wallowing in the pitfalls of the past has never helped anyone. It is not how many times you have fallen, but how many times you get up that counts.

During this period of humiliation, rejection and despair you would be wise to use the help of a dedicated counselor. This person has experienced these same feelings and will be the contact with reality that you need to see through another human being. This individual can help you understand that it is not the good, the righteous, the holy and the successful who are entitled to accept self and be worthy of God's love. Actually, only those who join the human race, admit their inadequacies, recognize that they are members of sinners annonymous and are aware of their unacceptability, can ever receive acceptance from God and man.

Acceptance of yourself, where you are, is the first step to receive God's power to move on and up. This is different from acceptance of yourself as yourself, from justification of your role playing, from the existential courage to be yourself, or the capacity to make the best of a bad situation. It is the acceptance of God's power to change you into the person He wants you to be and the acceptance of this real self. It is also the acceptance of what you have been as a disfigurement of what you can be. It is the willingness to enter into God's healing provided for you. Such forgiveness and acceptance is basic in your encounter with God.

As you share with a mature counselor who has gone through this process and is trained in the techniques of healing, you participate in the healing power of one who already accepts you while you still feel so unacceptable.

Here your "in spite of" will have to do with your deep sense of guilt, unworthiness and condemnation. *This is the beginning of learning how to be kind and merciful to yourself.* There is an inner child in your past to whom you must now be a good parent. There is no way for you to ever have self-acceptance outside a person-to-person relation. Personal self-rejection can never be overcome in anything less than the personal. *Things cannot forgive nor relate.* Along with the personal acceptance of someone else, you need to go beyond self-courage to the courage of confidence.

Here is the explanation of religious healing. Religion brings in the ultimate source of the One who accepts the unacceptable and brings His presence into life in such a way as to rework the past and redeem the person. Your acceptance by God; His forgiving and justifying reconciliation, is the only and ultimate source of the courage to be yourself; to overcome the past and to make today such a life as to fit in with God's destiny in the future. Anything else cannot overpower the nagging, gnawing discontent with role playing, non-being and the despair of self-condemnation. The courage to be yourself learns to reject everything but unceasing, exclusive commitment to God as the only means to abundant life and personhood.

Unless you have a genuine warm affection for yourself and a self-regard based upon knowing yourself, you can have no affectionate feeling toward others. It is not a matter of loving some illusions about yourself in the role you are playing. When you can accept your flaws, mistakes, blunders, offensiveness, frailties and limitations, you learn to accept the same in others. The main point is that only when you have the courage and strength to open your eyes to the unacceptable and ugliness in yourself and in others can you be aware of and associate with what is significant, healing, strong, beautiful, lovely and sound.

With a knowledge of your worth, the sense of inadequateness, littleness, emptiness and shallowness – the destructiveness so characteristic of the neurosis in every human being – is dissipated; and the person becomes free from inner bondage. You are free to give and to live without expectation of recognition and reward.

As you realize your basic strength you will not need to have appeals to give and live at your best. You will have a greater capacity to feel – wholeheartedly, deeply, richly and unselfishly because you feel strong enough to prevent your emotional reactions from spilling over and getting the best of you. Only in the courage to feel sadness, pain, discouragement and despair can you have the capacity for joy and happiness.

There is also a forgiveness of other people. Jesus taught that you are to ask forgiveness according to how you forgive others. Forgiveness of personal hurt and getting it out of one's system, means more than just stating it in another way. A woman once said: "I have made a change in my life. I used to feel so mean and hateful toward my uncle that if he had died, I wouldn't have gone to his funeral. But now I've seen the light; I'm willing to attend his funeral any time."

A man, ninety years of age, said that he did not have an enemy. Someone asked, "How come?" "I outlived everyone of the dad-blamed critters," he replied.

Neither of these attitudes overcome the personal hurt that keeps one from being right with God and man.

One day, in talking to a man about becoming a Christian, it was explained to him that if he did become a Christian, he must be willing to forgive his enemies, those who had wronged him and those who had hurt him in any way. He replied by saying: "I would like to be a Christian, but I just cannot find it in my heart to forgive a man who is my competitor in business and who has hurt me deeply."

If a man cannot forgive others because he wants to hold on to his hate, he cannot have God's forgiveness. If he had rather have his hurt than God's forgiveness, he has made a tragic choice.

Jesus told a parable to illustrate the spirit of forgiveness. A man who owed about $10,000,000 pleaded for mercy and received it. But when he met someone who owed him $17.00 he took him by the neck and choked him. His debtor asked for mercy, but was refused and put in prison. When this was told the king; " . . . his lord was wroth, and delivered him to the tormentors, 'til he should pay all that was due unto him. So likewise shall my heavenly Father do also unto you, if ye from your hearts forgive not everyone his brother their trespasses."

Jesus forgave Judas for his personal injury and betrayal. This is often the hardest thing, when someone who is so close and near seeks to destroy and injure, to forgive that one.

An imaginary story beautifully interprets that kind of forgiveness. The last act in the drama of human experience was over and the sons of man had all been gathered into the Father's house of many mansions. There was great joy among the heavenly host. Only one among the singing multitude seemed restless and unhappy. It was Jesus. He stood at the gate leading into the mansion. His eyes fixed on the far horizon of space, an expectant look of yearning masking His lovely face. One of the throng watched Him and asked, "Are you looking for someone?" Without turning his gaze from the horizon, the Lord replied: "Yes, I am looking for Judas." Jesus, the perfect man, could forgive Judas.

Forgiveness is the readiness to participate in personal healing, inspiration and redemption.

There is a willingness to accept the person as he or she is.

When one forgives a person for what he has done, then he accepts the person as he is. Everyone wants to shape-up a person in a different life, or to remake that life and then accept the person. But to relate oneself properly to another in the spirit of forgiveness means that one is willing to accept the person as he is and to work together in the cause of the family, business, church, or personal relationships.

CHAPTER XV

COURAGE IS THE PATH TO FEELING ENTHUSIASTIC

Enthusiasm is the most beautiful word on earth.

— Christian Morgenstern

Great designs are not accomplished without enthusiasm of some sort.

— Bovee

More and more men are beginning to cherish doubt and abhor pat solutions. They stand on the uncertain perimeter of tomorrow's mystery with fear and trembling, but they stand there convinced that they can make out the distant form of purpose on the hazy horizon. They are not awed by tradition — fifty years old or two thousand. They have participated in an age of affluence, while the preceding generation lived on war coupons and sloshed around on islands with oriental names. They have a sense of guilt about the abundance of things; they are in a deep, vicarious relationship to the hurting masses of the world — especially those in their own country. The knowledge explosion has bewildered them; they identify strongly with Dag Hammarskjold's idea of standing on the "frontier of the unheard-of." In the midst of so much to assimilate they are fighting not so much to know more but for the courage to be open to all that is about them. So they stand on the "frontier of the unheard-of." Todays keep yesterdays and tomorrows from colliding; but, paradoxically, they do collide in the hearts of sensitive men.Today many serious and unconventional men and women are standing on the peaks of Ur with the wind of the wilderness blowing in their faces, drawn like Abraham to the tents and plains of uncertainty. Their hope is in their committed following of these strange but redeeming frontiers. They want purpose, not propositions.

Man's ultimate desire is to have a meaningful life. This is the only way he can be enthusiastic about his life. Courage to discover that life is the path each must choose.

There are only two forms of moral courage: the courage to be yourself, and the courage to be a part of something other than yourself alone — and neither form is much good without the other; the first leading to eccentricity and selfishness, the second leading just as inexorably to the tyranny of the collective mass. Whatever life man has he wants it to be one he can share with others in an enthusiastic manner and speak with integrity.

You can eat balanced meals, exercise daily, keep your weight in bounds, and still die an untimely death just by failing to have a meaningful reason for living. In releasing a set of health rules, the famed heart specialist, Dr. Paul Dudley White, advised that there is a sense in which one should never retire, regardless of how long he lives. Said Dr. White, "Something interesting to do will solve, I believe, half the problems of today's aging people – physical, mental, spiritual, social, economic or financial."

The one who is in harmony with God, with himself and with others, is well-adjusted and equipped to cope with the ups and downs of life. But adjusted for what? Whatever else meaning to life is, one source of it is found in helping others. No activity is worthwhile that does not include this element.

Again, there must be the reminder that each life must be lived a day at a time. Find meaning for today and tomorrow will fit into place.

ONLY A DAY AT A TIME

Only a day at a time, Lord,
Please let me live.
Tomorrow's joys, tomorrow's hopes
Art Thine to give.
Forgive me, dear Lord
If I have been blind
To this day's ills. . .

— Mae Martin

This fourth quality of courage is learning the means for enthusiasm. Enthusiasm literally defined, is God being in you as the motivation for your life. Attitude and spirit which result from enthusiasm enable you to move through the doubts, drudgery and unpleasantness that are met in life.

In recent years the cynic, Los, had his day; and many decisions have been made from an existential point of view. An interpretation of this philosophy says that you can determine the direction and action of your life by deciding on the basis of the moment only. Later Epicureans seem to tell their generation, "Eat, drink and be merry" — happiness is the goal of life, grow it today while you can. It just didn't work out in the run of life. They disregarded God.

Feurbach explained God away in terms of the infinite desire of man's heart. Marx tried to do away with God in terms of an ideological attempt to rise above the given reality. Nietzsche made his attempt to rid the universe of belief in God by weakening the will to live. The consequence was the pronouncement that God was dead, and with His death the whole system of values and meanings for which man lived were to die.

Cynics are the noncreative existentialist. Today's cynics are not what the Greeks meant by the word. The Greek cynic was a critic of contemporary culture on the basis of reason and natural law. He was a revolutionist, a radical, a disciple of Socrates. Modern cynics are unwilling to follow anybody and in the process are so desirous to destroy everybody and their ideals that they end up destroying self. They do not believe in reason, have no criterion for truth, no set of values, no answer to the question of meaning.

Enthusiasm for life and in life can be a great motivation for moving through doubt to reality, from depression to normal function.

Enthusiasm is closely related to learning, use of your faculties and your purpose of life.

You must learn life's greatest gifts to be enthusiastic, and then use them to your own betterment. Anyone who experiences daily growth of his inner resources is going to be enthusiastic about life and his place in it.

No one was brought into this world dull, bored, or cynical. This happens when failures, despair, and disappointment have robbed one of the joy of living.

Miss Michael Drury has stated that somewhere between wanting to make the world over and wanting to hide from it is the balance that results in mature and adult enthusiasm. Enthusiasm literally means *God in you*. When God is within you, there is direction and motivation to overcome the begging to know what life means. You furnish the meaning by being yourself.

Sir Edward V. Appleton, the Scottish physicist whose research made possible worldwide broadcasting and brought recognition that went with the Nobel prize, was asked the secret of his discovery. He said that it was enthusiasm — it was even more important than professional skill. Unless a person has enthusiasm for his work, his life, his home and his religion, he will never undertake much and never achieve much.

Fortunes have been made, lives have been transformed, and destinies changed through enthusiasm. Discipline, determination, and patience are the fruits of enthusiasm in the reality of achievement and happiness.

Many of the pseudo-sophisticated ridicule enthusiasm. Anatole France properly answered them by saying, "I prefer the folly of enthusiasm to the indifference of wisdom."

Enthusiasm always accompanies a real zest for living. Find any man, woman, or youth, who is really enjoying life and you will see at the root of their enjoyment the spring of enthusiasm.

Emerson was reflecting on the joys and meaning of enthusiasm. He wrote: "Every great and commanding movement in the annals of the world is the triumph of enthusiasm."

Charles Kingsley must have been in like contemplation when he said: "We act as though comfort and luxury were the chief requirements of life, when all we need to make us really happy is something to be enthusiastic about."

The courage to be enthusiastic is in the life of every happy, meaningful and productive person. Dr. Norman Vincent Peale is such an apostle of enthusiasm. He has written an entire book entitled "Enthusiasm Makes The Difference."

How true are these words of Chalmer concerning enthusiasm: "It flourishes in adversity, kindles in the hour of danger, and awakens to deeds of renown."

You can have a wonderful time being yourself, but such a miserable existence if you try to be someone else.

Here's wishing you the best as you are freed from the bondage of the past to enjoy the freedom of being yourself — for this is life's greatest opportunity, to thine own self be true.

Thoughts To Consider

1. The courage to be true to yourself follows the guidance of your inner conscience.

2. Courage is the true self-affirmation in spite of what you have been.

3. Courage is the first of human qualities because it is the only quality which guarantees the others.

4. Conscience is the simplist and clearest expression of the exalted character and dignity of human life.

5. Courage is the faith to act that you might move from where you now are to where you are to be.

6. Acceptance of yourself is the first step to receiving God's power to move on and up.

7. The courage to forgive brings God's resources to make your life the highest and best.

8. Enthusiasm is literally God in you.

9. Whatever man may become is rooted in his will to be courageous.

10. The cardinal sin is not to have courage to be yourself.

11. Find the life that you can enthusiastically recommend to someone else and you will discover a higher life yourself.

12. The person who accepts himself can accept others.

13. The man who understands himself discovers others.

14. The man who is honest with himself can be honest with others.

No man is better than his lowest thoughts or highest aspirations. The person who is honest with himself is life's greatest victor.

ACKNOWLEDGMENTS

CHAPTER I
Psalm 37:4-6
Psalm 37:4

CHAPTER II
Matthew 7:1-5

CHAPTER III
Matthew 7:6
Luke 11:24-26 (Good News For Modern Man Translation)
Proverbs 26:11
II Timothy 1:7
Proverbs 27:19
John 14:6

CHAPTER IV
John 13:34
Mary Carolyn Davies, *This Is Friendship*

CHAPTER V
Luke 9:23
Matthew 7:7-8
Matthew 10:22
John 14:27

CHAPTER VI
Matthew 5:3
Matthew 10:22

CHAPTER VII

Matthew 19:19

Henry Drummond, *The Greatest Thing In All The World* (London: Collins) pp. 61-65

Matthew 7:13-14

Philippians 3:13-14

Roy Angell, *Baskets Of Silver* (Nashville: Broadman Press, 1955) pp. 60-62

CHAPTER VIII

II Timothy 1:7

Numbers 32:23

Matthew 7:2, Mark 4:24, Luke 6:38

Romans 8:28

I John 4:18

CHAPTER IX

Viktor Frankl, "The Will To Meaning," in *Are You Nobody?* (Richmond, Virginia: John Knox Press, 1967) pp. 23-31

Dale Carnegie, *How To Stop Worrying And Start Living*

CHAPTER X

John Milton (1608–1674) *Paradise Lost*

Romans 8:28

CHAPTER XI

Matthew 6:34

William Barclay, *The Gospel Of Matthew*, Vol. I (Philadelphia: Westminster Press, 1958) pp. 263-264

C. S. Lewis, *Mere Christianity*, (New York: The Macmillan Co., 1960) p. 105

II Corinthians 6:2

CHAPTER XII
   Matthew 16:25
   II Samuel 24:24
   Romans 12:2
   Oswald Chambers, *My Utmost For His Highest* (New York: Dodd, Mead and Co., 1962) p.134
   Romans 2:15
   I Samuel 24:5
   I Timothy 1:5

CHAPTER XIII
   Mark 9:23
   Galatians 2:20
   Matthew 14:4
   II Corinthians 4:2

CHAPTER XIV
   Matthew 6:14-15
   Matthew 18:23-35

ABOUT THE AUTHOR

Dr. Cort R. Flint shares the deep insights of his life in TO THINE OWN SELF BE TRUE. He has learned through the finest colleges, universities, seminaries and the university of hard knocks, that a man must be honest with himself before he can ever relate to others at his highest and best. Such honesty is necessary in the acceptance of other people and relating to them in work, at home, in the community and church. The suicide of his father when he was 11 years of age, the subsequent loss of the family holdings and the death of his high school sweetheart, embittered him toward life, God, and those who had wronged him and his family.

He was caught in the throes of self-pity and a negative mental attitude when he learned the philosophy of life which he presents in this book. Having been brought up in western Oklahoma during the depression, he has observed facets of life that many have never experienced.

Being active in sports, he learned that when the going gets tough, the tough get going. His wrestling team won the national A. A. U. championship.

As a young person, Dr. Flint worked on farms, ranches, and in business before he became involved in politics, the entertainment world, and a short career as a high school band director. He taught school while preparing for a law practice and his political future. Then a great change took place in his life which originated his service to his fellow man as an educator, administrator, consultant, chaplain and pastor.

He saw early in life, that the man who straddled the fence could never get his feet on the ground, and that the man who never stood for something would fall for anything.

This book will help any person in any walk of life take a fresh look into himself and enable him to enter a more meaningful life. Dr. Flint concludes that every person must be himself because he cannot be anyone else. This is life's greatest opportunity and man's highest privilege.